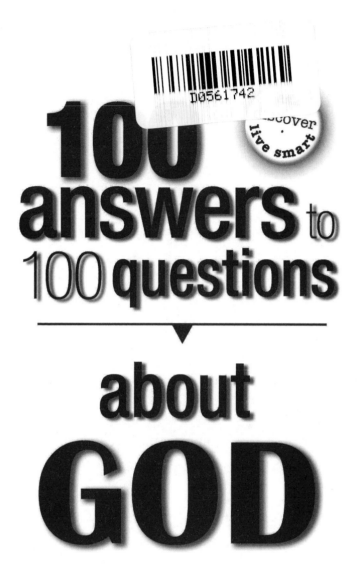

100 answers to 100 questions

about

GOD

Discover
live smart

D0561742

ask
discover
live smart

about

GOD

Christian
LIFE
A STRANG COMPANY

Most CHRISTIAN LIFE products are available at special quantity discounts for bulk purchase for sales promotions, premiums, fund-raising, and educational needs. For details, write Christian Life, 600 Rinehart Road, Lake Mary, Florida 32746, or telephone (407) 333-0600.

100 Answers to 100 Questions About God

Published by Christian Life
A Strang Company
600 Rinehart Road
Lake Mary, Florida 32746

www.strang.com

Scripture quotations marked GNT are from the Good News Translation, Second Edition. Copyright © 1992 by the American Bible Society. Used by permission.

Scripture quotations marked HCSB are from the Holman Christian Standard Bible®, Copyright © 1999, 2000, 2002, 2003 by Holman Bible Publishers. Used by permission. Holman Christian Standard Bible®, Holman CSB®, and HCSB® are federally registered trademarks of Holman Bible Publishers.

Scripture quotations marked THE MESSAGE are from *The Message: The Bible in Contemporary English*, copyright © 1993, 1994, 1995, 1996, 2000, 2001, 2002. Used by permission of NavPress Publishing Group.

Scripture quotations marked NKJV are from the New King James Version of the Bible. Copyright © 1979, 1980, 1982 by Thomas Nelson, Inc, publishers. Used by permission.

Scripture quotations marked NIV are from the Holy Bible, New International Version. Copyright © 1973, 1978, 1984, International Bible Society. Used by permission.

Scripture quotations marked NLT are from the Holy Bible, New Living Translation, copyright © 1996, 2004. Used by permission of Tyndale House Publishers, Inc., Wheaton, IL 60189. All rights reserved.

Cover design by Whisner Design Group, Tulsa, Oklahoma

ISBN 10:   1-59979-272-9
ISBN 13:   978-1-59979-272-9

BISAC Category: Religion/Christian Life/General

First Edition

08 09 10 11 12—9 8 7 6 5 4 3 2 1

Printed in the United States of America

"Stop fighting," he says,
"and know that I am God,
supreme among the nations,
supreme over the world."

Psalm 46:10, GNT

Contents

A Glimpse at God's Personality

The Purpose-Driven God

A Reliable Foundation

A Good Judge of All Characters

God Is Powerfully in Control

In All Places at All Times

The Lover of Your Soul

More Ins and Outs About God

Introduction

People are a curious bunch. You will find folks poking at things to see if they will move, pulling things apart to see how they work, and looking at something from all angles to see how it is made.

People ask questions because they are curious, too. Small children pester parents with why questions: Why is the moon so big when it comes up? Why do birds sit on telephone wires? Why do people have belly buttons?

You probably have questions, too. Some of those questions might be about God. If so, you are not alone. The Bible tells about a treasury official who had been in Jerusalem conducting some business for an Ethiopian queen. As he headed home, he took some time to read aloud from Isaiah. Philip, one of Jesus' disciples, came upon this man as he was reading. The man turned to Philip and asked, "Tell me, please, who is the prophet talking about, himself or someone else?" (Acts 8:34, NIV). This man had questions. By being available and helpful, Philip was able to introduce him to God. By meeting God in a new way, the official's life was changed. So why not let this book do for you what Philip did for the treasury official? Let this book introduce you to God in some new and interesting ways.

Within the pages of *100 Answers to 100 Questions About God*, you will find Bible verses, quotations, and inspirational thoughts drawn from the Bible to help answer your questions about God. You will also find some points for further consideration that might trigger more questions, but that is okay, too. God is not put off by your questions. He knows people are a curious bunch. Keep asking questions and looking for answers as you let this book give you a better understanding of God, His ways, and His plan for you.

> *I am convinced that human beings have an inborn desire for God. Whether we are consciously religious or not, this desire is our deepest longing and most precious treasure.*
> Gerald C. May
>
> *Everyone who asks, receives. Everyone who seeks, finds. And to everyone who knocks, the door will be opened.*
> Matthew 7:8, NLT

question

Who is God?

How would you reply if someone asked, "Who are you?" Rarely would it be enough to answer, "I'm Tim." You would probably answer with things that set you apart from someone else, such as your full name, a brief description of yourself, your relationship to another individual, or your position in a company. The same is true when asking, "Who is God?" To know who God is, you need to know what sets God apart from everyone else.

answer

Jesus once asked His disciples, "Who do people say I am?" His disciples responded with some strange answers—John the Baptist, Elijah, or one of the prophets reincarnated. In reality, Jesus is none of these. People came to the wrong conclusions by not asking Jesus directly about Himself. The same is true for you—and for God, too. You are the best source to tell others about yourself, just as God is the best source to tell others about Himself. And God has done just that. To find out who God is, you will need to go to the Bible.

Although the Bible does not contain a short definition of who God is, the chapters of Genesis say God is the personal Creator and Lord of the universe. He is a strong deliverer in the Book of Exodus. Leviticus portrays God as the object of His children's confession, worship, and service. The Book of Numbers reveals God as a great promise keeper and provider, whereas Deuteronomy describes God as the great lawgiver. Read Isaiah and you will discover God knows and controls the future. In fact, every page of the Bible shows another facet of God Himself. When you finally close your Bible at Revelation's affirmation of God as the righteous Judge of all humanity, you will have learned many things that set God apart from everyone else. And if anyone should ask you, "Who is God?" you will have a pretty good answer, too.

worth thinking about

▶ **People try to** define God with pithy phrases like "the prime mover," "a higher power," or "the absolute personality." Yet God is greater than any one-phrase definition.

▶ **People sometimes** draw conclusions about who God is from His actions. Those assumptions might be wrong, however, if they are not measured against what God says about Himself in His Word.

▶ **Reading about someone** presents a limited picture of that person. You learn more about folks by spending time with them. To better know who God is, spend time with Him.

> *The LORD alone is God;*
> *God alone is our defense.*
> 2 Samuel 22:32, GNT

2

question
▼
Is God real or merely a human invention?

Travelers in desert regions are warned about the dangers of dehydration. If the body loses too much water, the mind can malfunction. The imagination can conjure up something that is not really there. Yet the visions of people, places, smells, and sounds can be so compelling they appear real. Because the human imagination is so powerful, some have wondered if God is real or if He is merely an invention of the imagination like a desert mirage.

answer
▼

While the Bible presupposes the existence of God, Helen Keller experienced an awakening to the reality of God in her own life. Since the age of two, Miss Keller had been blind and deaf. Through the extraordinary efforts of tutors and assistants, she eventually learned to read and communicate with others. Not long after graduating from college, friends told Miss Keller about God and His love for her. Reportedly, she responded with joy, acknowledging that she had always known deep inside that someone was there, but she had never known His name. She had never known that that someone was God.

Helen Keller's innate sense of someone greater, wiser, bigger, and stronger than herself is not uncommon.

Every people group in the world has some idea of a supreme being. For everyone everywhere to think about God is more than imaginative coincidence. These thought patterns confirm God is not an invention of the mind or an imaginary friend sitting somewhere on a heavenly cloud. God is real.

Indeed the God of the Bible is bigger, stronger, wiser, and better than all human imagination. The writer of Ecclesiastes declared that God is the One who put the sense of something bigger into every person's heart in the first place. Jeremiah assured readers that those who seek God with their whole heart will find Him. And the psalmist proclaimed that only fools think there is no God. Is God real? Yes, He is.

worth thinking about

▶ If God were an invention of the imagination, He would not be God. Human imagination has limits. God is all-knowing, all-powerful, and present everywhere at once. He is limitless.

▶ You may not be able to prove God's existence with a science experiment, but you can discern His existence by studying the intricate design of the universe.

▶ God's existence is attested to by humanity's built-in moral barometer. When the conscience tells someone to do what is right, that sense comes from a greater moral being—God.

The basic reality of God is plain enough. Open your eyes and there it is!
Romans 1:19, THE MESSAGE

3

question

Who made God?

Look at a skyscraper with unusual rooflines or windows, and you will probably find yourself asking who the architect or builder might have been. Taste a fantastic dessert at a neighborhood supper, and you are liable to ask who made it so you can snag the recipe and re-create it yourself. Knowing who made something you enjoy, find tasty, or admire speaks to the human trait of curiosity. It is not surprising, then, for individuals to ask, "Who made God?"

answer

Consider this. With a bit of digging you could probably find the name of the builder who constructed your home or apartment. Some additional research might turn up the architect or landowner who planned the building. Behind every building, company, or development deal was a person—a prime mover or first cause—who decided to make that particular place or item a reality.

First causes influence people groups, too. When people trace their lineage back several generations, they often find points of relationship to other cultures or nationalities. Some Americans today are part Native American, Irish, and Eastern European because these people groups were the prime movers of the United States.

Yet when thought turns to who made God, causality hits a roadblock. The Bible says God is the prime mover of everything. Nowhere in the Bible is there any indication that God was made at all. The Book of Genesis indicates God is a bona fide first cause, the One responsible for all of creation. Exodus lists God's name as "I AM THAT I AM" or, loosely translated, "I am the One who was before all." God Himself is not bound by the element of time or causality. He is the only One "who is, and who was, and who is to come" (Revelation 1:8, NIV). God had no first cause, no prime mover. Instead, God exists, always has, and always will. No beginning. No end. No maker. Hard to fathom, but that's God.

worth thinking about

▶ Scientists believe that the universe once began with a big bang. The Bible indicates that the prime mover of that "big bang" was God Himself.

▶ The ancient Athenians deified men, ideas, and capacities. Yet even they knew they had missed the true first cause, for they built an altar "To an Unknown God."

▶ The Bible says God exists outside of time and space. That means He exists outside of creation and has no maker. Such mysteriousness keeps God permanently interesting to humanity.

> Since we are God's children, we should not suppose that his nature is anything like an image of gold or silver or stone, shaped by human art and skill.
>
> Acts 17:29, GNT

question

How big is God?

Size can be relative. When a child measures himself against a twenty-inch bicycle frame, the two-wheeled conveyance might seem huge. But the same frame placed alongside a full-grown basketball player would seem tiny. Likewise, when physical size, mental capacity, and spatial dimension are applied to God, one would be hard-pressed to quantify any of these measurements. Yet the Bible paints many verbal pictures to help folks grasp how big God truly is.

answer

In the final chapters of the Book of Job, God shed light on just how big He is. God revealed that He alone marked off the dimensions of the world, that He set the limits of daylight and darkness, and that He maintains a storehouse for all the snow and rain that will ever fall anywhere. God reminded Job that He is big enough to determine the movement of the stars and the timing of the seasons. He is big enough to hold back the sea, wrap the world in clouds, and care for everything He created.

But that is not all. The psalmist said God is so big He can measure all of the water in all of the world's oceans in the palm of one hand. He can hold all of the winds of the world in His other hand and still have room in that hand to hold all of the stars and planets—and more. God is huge!

Yet God is also small. Not in the sense of insignificant or tiny, however. No. God is small in the sense of being able to fill your entire being with all of Himself. God, who is larger than the universe, is big enough to have a wonderful plan for your life and yet small enough to fit inside your innermost spirit to guide, guard, and care for you.

So how big is God? The Bible says He is as big as you need Him to be—and then some.

worth thinking about

▶ **Nowhere in the Bible** is there an indication that God is limited in size, scope, or dimension in any way. He cannot be hemmed in or boxed out.

▶ **The apostle Paul** reminded his friend Timothy that God's immenseness extended to His words, too. They cannot be limited or their purposes contained by anyone except God Himself.

▶ **According to His** Word, God is so big His sphere of activity extends beyond the universe—beyond what anyone can think or even imagine. Now that is big!

> The LORD your God is supreme over all gods and over all powers. He is great and mighty, and he is to be obeyed. He does not show partiality, and he does not accept bribes.
>
> Deuteronomy 10:17, GNT

5

question
▼
Is there more than one God?

Carved stone images tower over an island in the Pacific. Huge pillars ring a spot on a British plain. A gilded statue sits cross-legged in a garden in Japan. A multi-columned temple covers acres of the Acropolis. Each of these places is a sacred site to adherents of certain religions. Because there are thousands of such shrines throughout the world, it might appear that there are many deities worthy of worship. But in reality, is there more than one God?

answer
▼

Though it might appear there are many deities, the Bible is very clear when it proclaims there is only one God with a capital G. To prove this point Elijah the prophet issued a challenge to some idol-worshiping Israelites.

During the time of King Ahab, the land of Israel experienced a terrible drought and famine. Many Israelites began worshiping a Canaanite god called Baal. Elijah knew this was wrong, so he challenged the worshipers of Baal to a contest to prove which god was the only true God.

On the day of the contest, two identical sacrifices were prepared. Then the worshipers of Baal started to pray, sing, dance, holler, and cut themselves with knives, asking Baal to prove himself real by starting a fire to burn up the sacrifice. From early morning until midday they continued, but nothing happened.

Then it was Elijah's turn. He soaked his sacrifice with gallons and gallons of water. Next, loudly enough so all could hear, Elijah prayed, "Lord, answer me so these people will know that You are the one true God." Immediately God sent fire down from heaven. It consumed the sacrifice and all the water that had been poured on and around it. When the people saw the fire, they fell on their faces, crying, "The LORD is God!" (1 Kings 18:39, CEV). Such an immediate, visible answer to a prayer settled the matter: there is only one God.

worth thinking about

▶ **As part of their** Shema, or creed of belief, Jews recite passages from the Book of Deuteronomy and the Book of Numbers that declare only the Lord God is the one true God.

▶ **Paul reminded** the Corinthians that there is only one God who created everything. People are to glorify and worship Him alone.

▶ **James commended** his readers for believing in God as the only true God. He declared even the demons of hell believe that fact—and shudder in fear.

> *Amid all the war and contest and variety of human opinion, you will find one consenting conviction in every land, that there is one God, the King and Father of all.*
>
> Maximus Tyrius

Who is God?

Look who's here: Mountain-Shaper! Wind-Maker! He laid out the whole plot before Adam. He brings everything out of nothing, like dawn out of darkness. He strides across the alpine ridges. His name is GOD, God-of-the-Angel-Armies.

AMOS 4:13, THE MESSAGE

6 question

Why does God have so many names in the Bible?

Throughout scripture, names have been important because of their underlying meaning and indication of a person's character, function, or destiny. Today some parents choose a child's name based on the way it sounds when spoken aloud. Others choose names that honor a friend or relative or that have significance in a family's ancestry. Later in life, some adults choose to change their name because of a life-altering event. So why does God have so many names?

answer

Each biblical name of God paints a verbal picture of God's person and work. For example, God's most common name in scripture is *Jehovah*, which means "the LORD." This name occurs almost seven thousand times in the Old Testament alone. Though sometimes occurring by itself, the name *Jehovah* is often combined with other terms to further describe God. *Jehovah Jireh*, *Jehovah Nissi*, and *Jehovah Shalom* are translated, respectively, "the LORD will provide," "the LORD my banner" and "the LORD is Peace." Each name combination reveals an essential aspect of God's person.

Another commonly used biblical name for God is *Elohim*. Usually translated "God," *Elohim* is used more than two thousand times in the Bible. It is the name given to God in the first verse of Genesis. Throughout scripture, this name proclaims God's power and might.

The Bible also uses everyday things like *lion, lamb, rock,* or *strong tower* as symbolic names for God. Most people instantly know that a rock is weighty, a lamb is gentle, a lion is fierce, and a strong tower would be a place of safety. By using these visual, well-recognized symbols as His name, God reveals Himself to people in ways they can understand.

God also uses names that are personal like *Abba Father*; names that denote His sovereignty like *Majesty, King of kings,* and *God Almighty*; and names that illustrate His "softer" side like *Shepherd* and *Comforter*. So, why does God have so many names? To show you a visible portrait of an invisible God.

worth thinking about

- ▶ *El* is also used in the Bible in name combinations for God. History's first sinner—Satan—used El Elyon in reference to the Most High God.

- ▶ Some of the names of God reflect a feminine quality. El-Shaddai denotes one who cares for another as a mother cares for her nursing infant.

- ▶ Some of God's names occur only once in scripture, as in the case of Sarai's Egyptian handmaid who was ministered to by "the One who sees" (Genesis 16:13, HCSB).

> LORD, *there is no one like you! For you are great, and your name is full of power.*
> Jeremiah 10:6, NLT

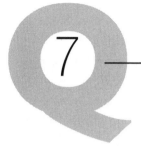

question

Is God only one God?

The Bible refers to God by many names. However, a commonly used biblical name for God has an unusual grammatical usage. **Elohim**, translated "God," is plural in its grammatical form, yet it is always paired with singular verbs. The Bible also speaks about a Holy Spirit of God and of Jesus as the "exact representation" of God. These words and phrases raise the question, is God only one God or is He a twin or triplet?

answer

Scripture is very clear when it states there is only one God. Yet the Bible also says that God is one God in three persons—God the Father, God the Son, and God the Holy Spirit.

The three dimensions of a book illustrate this three-in-one concept. Every book has height, width, and length. These three make up the whole book. They cannot be separated, yet they are not the same. This principle holds true with God. The three persons of God are only one God. They are equal in power, glory, and substance, but they are different and have distinct functions, too.

The Bible indicates that all three persons of God were present at creation when God said, "Let us make human beings in our image, to be like us" (Genesis 1:26, NLT). The three persons of God are seen in Matthew's Gospel, too. God the Father spoke audibly, and the Holy Spirit of God descended from heaven in the form of a dove as Jesus, the Son of God, was baptized in the Jordan River.

Throughout scripture, readers are assured that all three persons of God are eternal, all are holy, all are glorious, and all are all-knowing. All three are called *Lord* and *God*, too. The Book of Romans says that the three persons of God act as a unified whole. This triune God is unlike any other being in the whole universe. One God with three facets. A difficult concept, but an amazing God.

worth thinking about

▶ **Each person** of God is interrelated with each other person. The psalmists and the prophets proclaim the oneness of the Holy Spirit and the other persons of God.

▶ **The Gospels indicate** that Jesus, God the Son, is One and coequal with God the Father.

▶ **Jesus, God the Son**, came to earth as a person. He was fathered by the Holy Spirit and mothered by the Virgin Mary.

> *Go, therefore, and make disciples of all nations, baptizing them in the name of the Father and of the Son and of the Holy Spirit.*
> Matthew 28:19, HCSB

question

What does God know?

When a person applies for a job, an employer often asks for a résumé or a list of previous jobs to help determine whether the applicant knows enough to do the job well. Employers recognize that knowledge is an important aspect of better job performance. But what about God? If God were to submit a résumé for being the final authority on everything in the world, what would that résumé contain? What does God really know?

answer

The Bible declares that God knows everything in the past, present, and future. The Book of Job proclaims God's clear knowledge of the actions of all peoples. The Gospels stress God's knowledge of the needs of every individual. Throughout the Bible, whether in the prophetical books, the historical narratives, or the letters to early Christians, the Bible stresses God's knowledge of people's hearts and minds. He knows the inclinations of each person's heart, the thoughts harbored in the mind, and the words a person will say before they are even spoken.

God also knows the faults and failings of people. The prophet Jeremiah reminded the ancient Israelites that God was well aware of their secret thoughts, their lack of love for Him, and their desire to be like other ungodly nations. In the lives of individuals, the things hidden from human sight are still known to God. God knew what motivated Abimilech's behavior when he took Abraham's wife, Sarah, into his harem. God knew what was in Samuel's heart as he searched for a replacement king for Israel. God knew of Ananias and Sapphira's deception when they lied about their property's selling price.

God knows you, too. He knows everything about you— your talents and abilities, how many hairs are on your head, and how many days you will live on this earth. And in all of God's knowing, He also knows how to be just, loving, and caring to His children. God knows it all.

worth thinking about

- ▶ **Hagar thought** she was alone when Sarai cast her and her baby out into the desert, yet God knew right where she was and took care of her.

- ▶ **The Book of Job** says that God knows everything there is to know about the birds and animals—where they sleep, where they live, what they eat, and how they navigate their migration routes.

- ▶ **The Book of Genesis** says God knows every language on the planet, for He is the One who gave each nation its mother tongue.

> *Take comfort, and recollect however little you and I may know, God knows; He knows Himself and you and me and all things; and His mercy is over all His works.*
> Charles Kingsley

question

Is anyone smarter than God?

If you have ever felt that someone knew more than you did, you are not alone. It is a common sensation. Those with less or even more education or training sense there is someone out there with more street smarts or book knowledge than they currently possess. If this principle holds true for people, is it true for God, too? The Bible says God is knowledgeable. Yet is God truly smarter than Albert Einstein or Stephen Hawking? Is anyone out there smarter than God?

answer

According to the Bible, God is smarter than all of the smartest people in the world put together. Why? Consider this. Though brilliant by human standards, both Albert Einstein and Stephen Hawking learned their school lessons from books and teachers like most people do. Yet these men were very smart. They did not stop learning. Instead, they took the lessons they were taught and applied them in different ways to invent or discover new concepts.

But God is different. The Book of Isaiah declares God never had a human teacher because no person knows enough to be God's teacher. The Bible assures readers that God's knowledge and intelligence originate within Himself. God has never had to invent or discover anything, because He already knows everything. God never had to have a teacher because He is the source of all instruction and learning. God's knowledge is the pinnacle of intelligence.

The Book of Deuteronomy adds that God is so smart He knows secret things even the smartest person could not begin to understand. Though modern scientists look for ways to better predict severe storms and winds, the Book of Job declares that God is so smart He already controls the clouds and storms. He causes the lightning to flash whenever He wants it to flash. Daniel stated God is so smart He knows what lies hidden in the darkness. Only God can reveal these deep and mysterious things to people. No one is as smart as God is.

worth thinking about

▶ **Has it ever** occurred to you that nothing has ever occurred to God? He knows it all already and never has to consult an encyclopedia to confirm His facts.

▶ **Scientists say** the smartest human uses only a small percentage of the brain's total intellectual capacity. The Bible says God is not limited in this way.

▶ **People often** use a team approach to solve problems. Relying on one another's strengths, the plan comes together. God does not need a team. He knows what is best and does it.

> *God was smart when he made man. He made six holes in the head for information to go in, and only one for it to come out.*
> Wallace Johnson

question

Has God ever been foolish?

Restaurant servers sometimes deliver a main course on a heated plate to keep the meal warm. Customers are instructed to use caution and not touch the plate. Unfortunately, many customers immediately touch the plate anyway just to see how hot the dish is and pull back a burned finger as a result. Their response to the warning is foolish, yet people do foolish things time after time. But has God ever disregarded common sense? Has God ever been foolish?

answer

Though the Bible says God is never unwise, His ways can appear foolish to people. The apostle Paul observed that occurrence in ancient Corinth.

While in Corinth Paul preached to Jews and Greeks alike. He told Jewish listeners that Jesus was God's Son, their long-awaited Messiah, and that God sacrificed His Son on a cross to take away their sin and wrongdoing. This God-given message sounded like foolishness to those Jewish listeners. Paul then told the assembled Greeks that God Himself had come from heaven to live and work among people. Paul proclaimed God's desire for a personal relationship with individuals. To those educated Corinthians this God-given communiqué seemed like foolishness, too.

Likewise, it may appear to people today that it is foolish to place the care of this world, its plants and animals, oceans and lands in the hands of people. Yet this is exactly what God has done. He has also entrusted His message of hope and heaven to a world that fears death and hell. He has commissioned imperfect people to speak for Him and share the good news of His work in their lives so that more people will come to know and love Him.

Yet is God imprudent, irrational, stupid, or foolish to expect these things? No. The Bible says that what appears to people as God's foolishness is really God's wisest plan for the world. Rest assured God knows what He is doing. He has never been foolish, nor will He ever be.

worth thinking about

▶ **Is God foolish** to ask people to love their enemies when people find it hard to get along with their own friends and family members?

▶ **Is God foolish** to let people choose to ignore Him and make unwise choices? Is He foolish to wait for folks to seek His will and way?

▶ **Is God foolish** in granting forgiveness to the mistake-prone, in desiring fellowship with the unfaithful?

> *This foolish plan of God is wiser than the wisest of human plans, and God's weakness is stronger than the greatest of human strength.*
> 1 Corinthians 1:25, NLT

11 question

▼

Does God know everything that will happen in the future?

A toy manufacturer has made consistent sales from a strange black ball with the numeral eight on its side. The ball is not used for billiard games. Instead, by asking the ball a simple yes or no question and giving it a gentle shake, a triangular space on the bottom of the ball supposedly will reveal your future. Unfortunately, the ball does not know all. Its predictions rarely come true. But does God know everything that will happen in the future?

answer

▼

Jesus spent an afternoon teaching His disciples on a Galilean hillside. He reminded these close friends they did not need to worry about where their next meal would come from or what they would have available to wear. He didn't want His friends to fret about the things that bother so many people in the world, so Jesus simply reminded them, "Your Father knows what you need before you ask him" (Matthew 6:8, NIV).

What a wonderful and amazing truth. God knows the future. In fact, He knows what will happen to nations even before the nations are formed. Deuteronomy says God gave Moses a song to teach to the Israelites that foretold what they would do in the Promised Land years before they arrived at its borders. God said the song would serve as a lasting testimony to His foreknowledge and the faithlessness of His people.

David recognized God's foreknowledge when he penned Psalm 139. He wrote that God knew what he was going to say even before the words were spoken. Isaiah was well acquainted with God's knowledge of the future, too. He reminded the Israelites that God had spoken and announced what was going to happen to them. When God determined the time was right, He acted, and His prediction came to pass. Daniel told King Nebuchadnezzar that only God can reveal the mysteries of the end of time, for only God knows the future. The unknown future of nations, families, and individuals is fully known to God.

worth thinking about

▶ The Bible assures you God knows everything—everything about the past, the present, and the future.

▶ God told Moses in advance that the leaders of Israel would listen to him but that the king of Egypt would refuse to free the Israelites. These predictions both came true.

▶ Everything God announced beforehand through the Old Testament prophets that the Messiah would suffer was fulfilled to the last detail throughout the life, death, and resurrection of Jesus Christ.

> *Trust the past to God's mercy, the present to God's love, and the future to God's providence.*
> Saint Augustine of Hippo

question
Can God read minds?

Mind reading. Psychics claim they can do it. Many magicians profess the skill as well. And if a friend says the very thing you have been thinking, you might catch yourself proclaiming, "You read my mind!" Upon closer examination, however, you will probably find that psychics, magicians, and close friends are not true mind readers. Instead, they are good interpreters of some unconscious signals you have been sending. But what about God? Does He know what you are thinking right now?

answer

Many times throughout scripture, readers are assured of God's unfailing ability to discern people's thoughts. When King David was preparing to give his throne to Solomon, the old king called a meeting. In front of all his mighty men, overseers, tribal leaders, and warriors, King David urged Solomon to worship God and seek God's ways with his whole heart and a willing mind. Then the old king said something remarkable. In front of everyone, King David reminded Solomon that God can read every mind, know every thought, and discern what motivates those thoughts, too.

Other scriptures indicate that God knows not only people's thoughts and motives, but also the deep secrets hidden in the mind. For example, God knew the thoughts of a foreign king who misused holy objects from God's temple, the thoughts of a prophet as he anointed Israel's new leader, and the thoughts of the disciple who would betray Jesus.

The Bible also says God can know a person's thoughts no matter how many miles separate that person from God. That was news to the ancient Israelites who lived in captivity many miles from their homeland. Somehow, the people believed because they were far from home, God no longer knew what was going on in their lives. The prophet Ezekiel set that record straight. He declared God not only knew what the captives were doing and saying, but God also knew what was going through their minds. Indeed, God can read minds.

worth thinking about

- ▶ **God is no mere** magician or psychic. He is God. And He knows exactly what you are thinking right now.

- ▶ **According to** the Bible, God is the only One who can read minds. The devil does not have that ability.

- ▶ **Because God** knows your thoughts, He also knows your unspoken needs, your unspoken prayers, and your unspoken love for Him.

> *Learn to know the God of your ancestors intimately. Worship and serve him with your whole heart and a willing mind. For the LORD sees every heart and knows every plan and thought.*
> 1 Chronicles 28:9, NLT

question

Will God give guidance to everyone who asks?

Anyone wishing to drive across this country could probably use a little guidance. While travelers might know the general geography of their trip, online maps, tour guides, road atlases, state maps, and global positioning gadgets would be helpful as travelers move from one location to another. However, along the road of life a GPS system is of no use. Where, then, can a person find direction and assistance? Will God give guidance to everyone who asks?

answer

God's guidance is necessary for life because people do not always know what is best. Sometimes others cloud the real issue, and an incorrect decision can be made. The ancient Israelites experienced this firsthand. God had promised to guide the Israelites no matter what. All He required in return was their faithfulness to Him and His plan. However, when the Israelites came to Canaan, the people listened to several men who said the country was dangerous. They urged the Israelites to turn back despite God's promises. Because the Israelites followed the directions of fearful men instead of God's guidance, they wandered in the desert for forty years.

Yet the Bible includes examples of those who asked for God's guidance and followed it, too. On one of Paul's missionary journeys, God guided Paul in a dream and told him to go another way. Abraham's servant asked for God's guidance when he sought a wife for Isaac. When God directed him to a well, he found Rebekah.

However, God's guidance comes with limitations. Much as a family keeps some secrets—a family recipe, the combination for the safe, the location of important papers, and so forth—God also has family secrets, giving guidance primarily to His children. For those who are repentant, humble, and willing to obey His plan and purpose, God grants marvelous guidance.

worth thinking about

▶ **When Jonah ran** from God and sailed off into a storm, the non-Jewish crew cast lots to find out who was responsible for the calamity. God guided them to Jonah.

▶ **God sometimes gives** unsolicited guidance to His children. As Moses tended sheep for his father-in-law, Jethro, God's voice spoke from the burning bush, sending him back to Egypt.

▶ **God's written words** in the Bible can also be used for guidance. The psalmist, Isaiah, and Peter all experienced the light God's Word can cast on life's path.

> *When Christ's abiding presence becomes our guide, then guidance becomes an almost unconscious response to the gentle moving of his Holy Spirit within us.*
>
> Bob Mumford

14

question

Can people hide anything from God?

A long-eared bunny rabbit is suspected of hiding Easter eggs for youngsters to find. Folks stash birthday and Christmas presents in secret places to keep them safe from prying eyes. Misers are accused of hiding money under mattresses. Government operatives keep items of national security hidden from reporters or spies from other countries. It seems people spend a lot of time hiding a variety of things in different ways and places. But can anyone hide anything from God?

answer

The writer of Hebrews said, "Nothing in all creation is hidden from God's sight. Everything is uncovered and laid bare before the eyes of him to whom we must give account" (Hebrews 4:13, NIV). Some people in the Bible underestimated the implications of this truth, including Ananias and Sapphira.

Early Christians often lived together in communities. They shared whatever they had with one another so that no one would go hungry or be without housing. The Bible says that a man named Ananias and his wife, Sapphira, lived within one such community. The couple sold a piece of property but then made a big mistake. Ananias decided he did not want to give all of the money from the sale to the community, so he lied and told his wife to lie, too. He brought part of the money to the community leaders, but claimed it was the full amount. God knew that Ananias was lying, and He revealed the deception to Peter. When Peter confronted Ananias with his lie, the Bible says that Ananias immediately fell to the floor and died. Three hours later when Sapphira met with Peter and lied about the sale price of the property she, too, died instantly. This couple thought they could hide something from God and ended up losing their lives.

The Bible says that God fills the heavens and earth so there is no place for anyone to hide anything from Him. He knows. He sees. He loves. And He always will.

worth thinking about

▶ **Adam and Eve** were the first people who tried to hide something from God. They thought they were the only two who knew about their wrongdoing, but God knew, too.

▶ **Bad habits** might be able to be hidden from friends and family, but bad habits can never be hidden from God.

▶ **The Bible says** God knows the thoughts that are in your heart and mind before you ever give voice to them.

> *Nothing is, or can be, hidden from the eye of God, to which all things are naked and open....God sees every thing truly.*
> Matthew Henry

question

Does God have a reason for allowing human suffering?

The evening television news streams video clips and still photos of atrocities around the globe. Starving children, bodies mutilated by unforeseen land mines, bombed-out buses and trains, ambulances laden with the injured, war-ravaged cities—the images are endless. You might be able to change the channel on your television set, but that will not change the reality of a world plagued by hardship and horror. Does God really have a reason for allowing such human suffering?

answer

God always has a reason for what He does and for what He allows, though people may not always understand those reasons. Biblical accounts indicate human suffering happens when there is a clash between good and evil. Job's suffering was caused by Satan as a means to test and try him. Though people plead with God to end their suffering, the psalmist said God may not stop suffering when people ask. God is aware of suffering, the psalmist declared, but sometimes He allows it to happen to make people stronger, stouthearted, or bold in their faith.

The Bible also says God is powerful enough to wipe out all human suffering with one word, but He allows suffering because He loves people. That may sound strange, but if God were to destroy those who do wicked, wrong things to other people, He would have to destroy everyone because the Bible says everyone has committed some kind of wrongdoing, some kind of sin.

But God loves people. He does not want folks to die without having a relationship with Him. So God "proves His own love for us in that while we were still sinners Christ died for us" (Romans 5:8, HCSB). God not only lets humanity live, He gives folks a way to end human suffering by offering everyone a changed heart. In God's hands human suffering can serve a positive purpose. Suffering can be a reminder of humanity's need for God's touch on every heart.

worth thinking about

▶ **Job spoke out** of personal experience to those who are suffering, reminding them that God will bandage and heal the wounds and injuries of each hurt.

▶ **The Bible says** that God is aware of all human suffering and will one day bring it all to an end when He comes to judge the world.

▶ **Paul reminded** the Corinthian believers that their perseverance in suffering could become a means for comforting other people who were also having a tough time.

> *God whispers to us in our pleasures, speaks to us in our conscience, but shouts in our pains: it is His megaphone to rouse a deaf world.*
> C. S. Lewis

What does God know?

God made our ears—can't he hear? He made our eyes—can't he see? He scolds the nations—won't he punish them? He is the teacher of us all—hasn't he any knowledge? The LORD knows what we think; he knows how senseless our reasoning is.

Psalm 94:9–11, GNT

16

question

How has God shown His wisdom and knowledge?

Television game shows often pit contestants against one another to determine who has the greater knowledge of a cluster of trivia questions. Sometimes adults go up against other adults, and sometimes adults find themselves competing with children. When the game ends, there will be some losers. But ultimately, the television audience will applaud the contestant who had the most knowledge. Because God does not participate in television game shows, how has God shown His wisdom and knowledge?

answer

The Bible indicates God often shows His wisdom and knowledge through the lives of His children who spend time actively seeking Him. During the time of Daniel, the Babylonian king Nebuchadnezzar had a troubling dream. None of his magicians could help him remember the dream or interpret it for him. So Daniel and his friends began to pray. God miraculously explained the king's dream to Daniel, revealing the knowledge Daniel needed only after Daniel spent time in prayer seeking God.

Solomon recognized the importance of the prayer principle, too, and acted on it. When he became king, Solomon asked God for help, admitting his inadequacy to rule the nation of Israel. God mightily answered Solomon's prayer.

God will give His wisdom and knowledge liberally to all who ask. He will neither belittle the one asking nor find fault with any question. The only caveat to God's follow-through is a belief that God will answer. If someone asks for God's wisdom and does not really believe that God will answer, God will not share His wisdom with such a person.

There are deep riches to be found in the wisdom and knowledge of God. These treasures can be mined through prayer, too, for God will graciously "give wisdom to the wise" (Daniel 2:21, NIV).

worth thinking about

▶ **The dependent relationship** between plants and animals, the power that holds atoms together, all things in creation attest to God's wisdom and knowledge.

▶ **History confirms** God's wisdom and knowledge, for the Bible says God predetermines the rise and fall of nations, their rulers, and the limits of their borders.

▶ **The apostle Paul** told the Colossians that all the treasures of God's wisdom and knowledge are hidden in Christ. These treasures can be revealed through a personal relationship with Him.

> *Where God gives a sincere desire and inclination to know him he will give that knowledge. It is God himself that gives a heart to know him, else we should perish forever in our ignorance.*
>
> Matthew Henry

17

question

Can people know what God knows?

Because God knows everything, He does not have to go to school to learn anything. But people are different. People have gaps in their knowledge and need to go to school to fill in those gaps. Yet learning everything taught in grade school, high school, college, graduate school, and technical school will still not add up to what God knows. So is there a way for people to learn everything? Can people know what God knows?

answer

Theologians disagree on this question. Some say if God's knowledge were fully comprehensible through human reason, God would not be God. Others suggest that no one can ever know what God knows because God's mind is so vast it would take an eternity to mine God's knowledge base. But other scholars counter that God has made humanity in His image and that the human brain has untapped resources. Therefore, people might be able to learn and retain more and more of the knowledge that God knows.

The Bible seems to indicate that all sides of this debate may be right. According to Proverbs, all human knowledge proceeds from God. For anyone to seek knowledge apart from God is futile. Yet the prophet Amos assured readers that people can know more than simple school-book lessons. Daniel asserts that God will reveal His thoughts and knowledge about life's mysteries to people. Indeed because God's knowledge is complete, James says people should request God's knowledge when they are in trouble or puzzled about something.

Though God's knowledge is attainable right now, the Bible stresses that that knowledge is limited in its fullness and scope. The apostle Paul reminded the Corinthians that life on earth is a dim reflection of what is to come. Though people can know some of what God knows now through prayer and study of the Bible, full knowledge of what God knows will not come until folks see God face-to-face.

worth thinking about

▶ **God has stamped** His image on every heart and implanted a piece of eternity in every soul so that people will seek Him to know what He knows.

▶ **The Bible says** if you want to know what God knows you should remember, "God gives wisdom, knowledge, and joy to those who please him" (Ecclesiastes 2:26, NLT).

▶ **Human reasoning** cannot fully comprehend God's knowledge. Isaiah says God's thoughts and ways are higher than people's thoughts and ways.

Were the works of God readily understandable by human reason, they would be neither wonderful nor unspeakable.
Thomas à Kempis

18

question
What is God like?

Your driver's license gives some information about you. Your photograph is your visible likeness. Your personal details of height and eye color add some particulars to the mix. The address lines help fill in extra pieces of information so that anyone examining your driver's license would know quite a bit about you. But God does not have a driver's license. To find out what God is like, the Bible is the best place to start.

answer

From the beginning of Genesis to the end of Revelation, the Bible tells you something about God on every page. Isaiah reveals God's all-knowing nature, and Exodus shows God's compassionate side. God's faithfulness shines through in Numbers, and His goodness and mercy are sung throughout Psalms. Jeremiah makes known a great God, while Ephesians celebrates God's grace and glory. Zephaniah paints a picture of a righteous Father who rejoices over His children. And Job hails God's majesty and sovereignty over all the earth.

Some overarching characteristics of God resonate throughout the Bible, too. God's love is shown repeatedly. His holiness, perfection, and righteousness cannot be missed. His forgiveness and forbearance go hand in hand in every book and chapter of the Bible. He willingly gives, redeems, and restores. He is trustworthy in all His ways. His wisdom and knowledge exceed all of humanity's wisdom. And His power is mightier, stronger, and greater than anything in the universe.

But as you read the Bible do not miss the softer side of God, too. He is a giving God who bestows blessings on His children. He is a listening God who hears the prayers of His people. He is an invisible God who made Himself visible to people through Jesus Christ. He is a God who understands suffering because His Son died on a cross. And He is a welcoming God who opens the gates of heaven to all who follow His ways.

worth thinking about

- ▶ **God is a purposeful** being. The Bible says His plan and purpose stand forever. They cannot be thwarted by human beings or evil powers.

- ▶ **Scripture says** God is present everywhere at all times. He transcends time and space.

- ▶ **God is not** like anything people can make with their hands—not like any statue, any portrait, or any crafted item. He is uncreated and the source of all life.

> *People grow up with all sorts of notions of what God is like. . . . Because of Jesus, however, we no longer have to wonder how God feels or what he is like. When in doubt, we can look at Jesus to correct our blurry vision.*
>
> Philip Yancey

question

Does God have emotions like people do?

Depending on the day, the moment, or the situation, people can experience a vast array of emotions. A heart-wrenching greeting card commercial can send someone into tears of joy. An intense discussion can cause anger to surface. A roller coaster can instill fear with an unexpected drop, twist, or turn. An individual could feel all these emotions in one day. But God is different. He is changeless. So, does God have emotions like people do?

answer

The answer to this question is yes—and no. The Bible indicates that God does have emotions. The Old Testament prophets wrote that God takes joy and delight in His people. Zephaniah said God sings with joy over His children. The Book of Hosea resounds with a God full of love. The Gospels portray God as compassionate and kind. And the Book of Lamentations and the letters of Paul show the emotion of mercy in God's dealings with people.

God also exhibits jealousy. In the Book of Exodus, God Himself reminded Moses and the Israelites that He is a jealous God, not wanting to share His children's love with anyone or anything. In fact, one of God's names is "Jealous." The Bible also portrays God as expressing anger when His children repeatedly disobey as well as showing pity when His children suffer.

But God's emotions are different from human emotions. Human emotions can be positive or negative, but God's emotions are always positive. For example, people may feel fear or rejection when love is not returned. God merely pours out more love if His first attempts at love are spurned. People may allow anger to grow in destructive ways. The Bible says God's anger is always exhibited righteously. People also may feel incorrect emotions, like a sense of security when disaster is looming. God's emotions will always be perfectly timed and flawlessly enacted.

worth thinking about

▶ **Because God controls** His emotions, the Book of James reminds God's children to control their emotions, too.

▶ **Human emotions** are important in the life of faith. The Bible says God's people are to use their emotions to be feeling and caring toward others.

▶ **Human emotions** are changeable. In certain circumstances, they can be misinterpreted, too. God's emotions are stable, unchanging, with no hint of misunderstanding.

> *God is a God of emotion, and if he observes mathematics, it is mathematics set to music, and his figures are written, not in white chalk on blackboards, but by a finger of sunlight on walls of jasmine and trumpet-creeper.*
> Thomas De Witt Talmage

20 question
Is God always truthful?

When a person is called to give a statement in a trial, the bailiff will ask the individual to swear to tell the truth—the whole truth and nothing but the truth. To determine someone's innocence or guilt, all testimony must be truthful. Yet some folks are not completely truthful under oath. They may color their testimony to protect someone they love. Because God loves His children, would He ever lie to protect them? Is He always truthful?

answer

God's nature is built on goodness, truth, love, and faithfulness, so it is impossible for God to be false in any way. The Book of Numbers says God does not lie, Isaiah says God speaks the truth, and the psalmist says God is characterized as truth. God's names reflect His truthfulness, too. Jeremiah refers to Him as "the true God," and the Psalms often call Him "the God of truth."

But there is more. The Book of Romans proclaims God's truthfulness in contrast with the falseness of earthly rulers and the false gods of other nations. And God's truthfulness is demonstrated through the life and work of Jesus Christ. The Gospel of John reminds readers that Jesus, God's only Son, was the tangible revelation of God in human form. Thus, God's truthfulness was defined by the person and work of Jesus Christ, for no other man could claim, "I am the way, the truth, and the life" (John 14:6, NKJV).

God's truthfulness in character is also seen in the constancy of His words. Paul's letter to Titus resounded with the message that God's words are consistently true and reliable. The psalmist said that because God is truth His promises are also truthful and dependable. And John's Gospel gives God's children hope as it reminds readers that God's people can rest securely in God's truthfulness. No matter the circumstances, the Bible declares God will always be true to His nature. He will always be truthful no matter what.

worth thinking about

▶ **Because God** is completely truthful and reliable in everything, His written word in the Bible is a dependable basis for the life of faith.

▶ **God's truthfulness** forms the framework for His covenants with people. Because He is truthful, He can be trusted to fulfill His promises.

▶ **Because God is truthful**, the teachings of Jesus are truthful, too. Jesus—God on earth in human form—is as truthful and trustworthy as God the Father.

> *I place myself in your care. You will save me, LORD; you are a faithful God.*
> Psalm 31:5, GNT

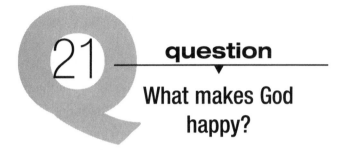

question

What makes God happy?

Happiness can be a fleeting feeling for some people. If circumstances and situations are good, they are happy, but even a minor irritation can force happiness out of the picture. With God, it is different. The Bible uses terms like *blessed, delighted*, and *joyful* to bring God's view of happiness into focus. And because God is God, His happiness is not affected by circumstance or situation. When God is happy, it is a long-lasting, deep-down delightedness, no matter what.

answer

So what makes God happy? The answer is simple. You do! That is what the Bible says. God is delighted and blessed in His children.

Think of it this way. When a sports team makes it to the finals and the cameras zoom in on one of the players who shouts, "Hi, Mom!" you can be assured that the athlete's mother is deep-down happy. She is not upset over a torn uniform or a dirt smudge on a smiling face. She looks beyond all that because she sees her child. She responds to that child with delight, with smiles and laughter, and with unbridled happiness.

God is like that, too. Tucked into the Bible are reminders and promises that God your Father is with you, that He is strong and mighty, and that He takes great delight in you and all of His children. In fact, the prophet Zephaniah declared that you make God so happy He sings over you with joy.

But that is not all. Moses reminded God's people that God finds happiness in His children especially when they obey Him and keep the commands in His Word. Solomon wrote that God is happy with those who are honest and honorable. The psalmist added that God is delighted with those who hope in His unfailing love. And the Gospels record God's happiness with those who are trustworthy.

Many things make God happy, but you are one of the best. You are one of God's deep-down delights—just by being His child.

worth thinking about

▶ **The Bible assures** you that God's joy and happiness can spill over into your life every day and become your unending source of strength.

▶ **The psalmist rejoiced** in God's happiness because he knew that when God is happy with you, God is also always ready to deliver you from any trouble.

▶ **Solomon knew** firsthand that God does not keep His happiness all bottled up. Those who make God happy will receive wisdom, knowledge, and joy from God in return.

> *Joy can be the echo of God's life within you.*
> Duane Pederson

22

question

Does God ever suffer?

Some people seem to get the best jobs and the nicest cars. They live in fabulous places and own all the great toys. These folks never seem to suffer like the rest of the world, either. The Bible says God's home in heaven is just like this. No trouble, no pain. Great home, great climate, great neighbors. So if the favored few on earth never suffer, how about God? Does He ever suffer?

answer

Amazingly enough, the Bible indicates that God does suffer—for several reasons. At the time of Noah, the Book of Genesis says that God was heartsick and full of pain because of the failures and wrongdoing of people. Samuel records God's grief over making Saul king over Israel. And Jeremiah likened God to a parent who suffers pain when His children suffer or do wrong.

Yet God also identifies and feels with the sufferings of others, too. Isaiah said that when the Israelites suffered at the hands of their oppressors, God suffered, too, and personally rescued them. The Bible indicates it was God's suffering that caused Him to send prophets and messengers repeatedly to the Israelites to urge them to turn back to Him. Isaiah also said that God felt pity and grieved for the ungodly nations that constantly terrorized Israel, for He knew what their outcome would be.

The Bible also says God's plan of salvation caused Him to suffer, too. In the Gospels, readers are told that God suffered in giving His Son to the world as a sacrifice for sin. God suffered along with His Son when the crowds did not believe His message. He suffered with Jesus when the religious leaders refused to listen to Him. And He suffered, too, as Jesus' disciples misunderstood the reason for His coming. Because of God's compassion and love, He suffers the hurts of His children.

worth thinking about

▶ **According to the** Gospels, there is a shared element in God's suffering with His Son at the time of Christ's trial, crucifixion, and death. What Christ felt, God suffered, too.

▶ **God's children** are called to share in God's suffering. Both Paul and Peter indicate that God's suffering is an example all Christians should follow.

▶ **The Bible also** says that Jesus' attitude of nonretaliation when He suffered should be the hallmark of God's children's attitudes toward suffering, too.

O brothers, let us leave the shame and sin of taking vainly, in a plaintive mood, the holy name of Grief! . . . By the grief of One came all our good.
Elizabeth Barrett Browning

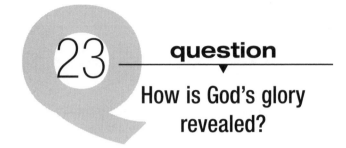

23

question

How is God's glory revealed?

If you possess an instinctive ability, you probably have proved yourself and that talent to others in some way. For example, an artisan will create a work of art that others admire. A gifted public speaker will keep an audience entertained and informed. A talented mechanic will tweak an engine to top efficiency. Because God has an innate characteristic of glory, how does He prove that character trait? How is God's glory revealed to people?

answer

Glory—the distinctive feature of God's presence—is characterized in the Bible as a state of splendor or a visible, majestic brilliance that inspires awe or fear. When Moses asked to see God's glory, God said human eyes could not behold all His glory. However, God allowed His glory to pass by as Moses hid in a protected crevice, covered by God's hand. When Moses rejoined the Israelites in the valley below, the Bible says the people were afraid of him, for his face still shone with the glory of God. Ezekiel also saw a portion of God's glory as he sat in Babylon. He likened the visible splendor of God's glory to a bright rainbow against a dark storm cloud.

God's glory has been revealed in the life of Jesus Christ, too. Luke says the shepherds in Bethlehem experienced God's glory when the angels appeared with the news of Jesus' birth. Hebrews says Jesus was the exact representation of God's nature and a visible manifestation of God's glory in human form. And when Jesus was about to be crucified, John's Gospel says that He commended Himself to God so that God would receive glory.

God's glory is still revealed today, if you look for it. The Book of Romans says God's glory is visible in creation. And the Psalms declare the sunshine is a hint of God's glory, lightning is a flash of His glory, and God's glory is on tour throughout the skies every day and every night.

worth thinking about

▶ God does not share His glory with just one or two special individuals or one chosen nation. The Bible says God's glory is on display for the whole world.

▶ As the Israelites wandered in the desert, they experienced God's glory daily. As they set up their tent of worship, God's glory would descend on the tent and remain there.

▶ The Bible says God's children are reflectors of God's glory, too. By growing and becoming more like Christ, your life can reflect God's glory to others.

> The Lord—who is the Spirit—makes us more and more like him as we are changed into his glorious image.
>
> 2 Corinthians 3:18, NLT

24 question

How does God's holiness affect His relationship with people?

Most people could not walk in the front door of the White House and expect to see the president of the United States at a moment's notice. The president's powerful position as a national leader prohibits such familiarity. Yet a few folks have easy access to the commander in chief. Family members and close cabinet advisers possess that power because of their relationship to the president. Likewise, God's holiness affects folks' ability to gain easy access to Him, too.

answer

God's holiness—His ethical, honorable, moral excellence expressed through His words and actions—sets God apart from all other beings. The Bible stresses, "There is no one holy like the LORD" (1 Samuel 2:2, NIV). Only God is divinely righteous deep down in His character, temperament, and personality. And because God is so holy, so righteous, and so divinely excellent, His holiness affects His relationship to people. Why?

According to the Bible, God's holiness makes willful wrongdoing objectionable to Him. The Old Testament acknowledged that God does not tolerate any wrongdoing in His presence. The prophets insisted that God's eyes are too pure to look at anything evil. The New Testament expanded this thought, depicting God as pure light. Willful wrongdoing—what the Bible calls "sin"—was characterized as darkness. Since God is light, He cannot have a relationship with darkness, with anyone who willfully makes wrong choices. In fact, it is as impossible for God to tolerate sin as it is for you to tolerate water in your lungs. Lungs exist to breathe air, not water. Likewise, God exists in holiness and light, not in sin and darkness.

God's holiness puts limitations on His relationship with people. Yet the Bible says there is a way to overcome the limitation of darkness and attain a close relationship with God. How? By seeking God's forgiveness.

worth thinking about

▶ **God's holiness** affects His relationship to people when they worship. The Bible says worshippers must have forgiven, prepared hearts that are motivated to serve God.

▶ **God's holiness** is to be seen in His people. Leviticus says God's children are to be holy as God Himself is holy.

▶ **God's holiness** necessitates humanity's dependence on Him for forgiveness from wrongdoing and cleansing of the heart. Holiness is not present in any heart unless God places it there.

> *Holy, holy, holy! Though the darkness hide Thee, though the eye of sinful man Thy glory may not see, only Thou art holy; there is none beside Thee, perfect in pow'r, in love, and purity.*
>
> Reginald Heber

question

▾

Is God good and kind to everyone?

The Bible contains stories that can bring God's goodness into question. His instructions to the Israelites to destroy everything in a city might seem cruel and unkind to readers today. Yet upon closer inspection, if the Israelites had followed those instructions completely, there would have been far-reaching positive effects for all concerned. In the end, God's instructions would have been good for all. So, even if it looks otherwise, is God always good and kind to everyone?

answer

▾

The answer to this question is both yes and no. According to the Bible, God is intrinsically good and kind by nature. God demonstrates His goodness daily through His actions, His love, and His promises. His commands are innately good, and the Bible says God will bring good out of unfavorable circumstances.

The Bible praises God's kindness to those who love Him and keep His commandments and to those in deep trouble, too. God kindly sympathizes with human weakness and actively seeks to restore those who are in need. The Book of Genesis reveals God's goodness and kindness hard at work in Joseph's life. After years of slavery and imprisonment, Joseph finally found himself elevated to the position of second-in-command to the ruler of Egypt.

However, there are limits to God's goodness and kindness. Those who choose to do wrong and live outside God's commands will not experience the breadth of goodness and kindness that is available to those who love God and do what He says. The Bible declares that God will be good and send rain on the just and the unjust, but only His children can request and receive showers of blessings in the form of well-being, protection, or guidance. God is kind to all people, offering everyone a means to escape eternal punishment. But only God's children will receive God's parental compassion, His tender mercies, and His abundant kindness for eternity.

worth thinking about

▶ **Humanity's ability** to show kindness and goodness comes only as a reflection of God's kindness and goodness. Without God, people would not know how to be kind or good.

▶ **The Bible says** that a person's failure to acknowledge or remember God's kindness is a wrong, sinful act.

▶ **God's goodness** and kindness are magnified through the sacrifice of His Son. Jesus' blood washes God's wrath and judgment away from a person's life, leaving grace and forgiveness behind.

> *God is too kind to do anything cruel, too wise to make a mistake, too deep to explain himself.*
> Charles R. Swindoll

What is God like?

God is Spirit, and only by the power
of his Spirit can people worship
him as he really is.

John 4:24, GNT

26

question

▼

Does God get angry or upset?

It never fails. You are late for an appointment, and traffic comes to a standstill. After fifteen minutes, you are angry and upset—at the situation and at yourself for not choosing another route to begin with. Folks often find themselves in frustrating situations. Some days it is easier to shed the annoyances and let things slide. But on other days, anger can quickly blossom. Since God is untouched by inconveniences, does He ever get upset? Does God ever get angry?

answer

▼

Anger, as an emotion, goes deeper than frustration or upset, becoming a strong feeling of displeasure brought about by an injury, injustice, or wrong. The Bible says God does get angry. Unlike people, however, God's anger is always justifiable and controlled. There is no lashing out or fit of rage. Though Nahum says God's anger is fearsome, the prophet Habakkuk declared God's anger is consistent with His righteousness and mercy. Jeremiah assured readers that God's anger will always fulfill God's purposes. And the Book of Exodus demonstrates God's anger as a short-lived last resort to continued wrong.

So what brings about God's anger? The books of the Kings and Chronicles indicate that disobedience and disloyalty to God's way will bring about His anger. The Book of Numbers adds that the idolatry and unbelief of the ancient Israelites triggered God's anger against them. The New Testament takes this concept further, declaring that a person's unbelief or rejection of Jesus as Son of God and Savior also brings God's wrath on that individual. And according to Jude, God's judgment against the ungodly is a sign of His anger toward those who oppose Him.

Other things can stir God's anger, too. Matthew's Gospel resounds with cautions about pride, arrogance, and hypocrisy. The prophet Malachi warned against injustice. God still gets angry today when His purposes are opposed, His messengers rejected, and His character defamed.

worth thinking about

▶ **God's anger** has a result. When God shows His anger, His holiness, and greatness will be revealed.

▶ **God's anger** has a purpose. Though God will show His anger to His children, it will ultimately purify and restore His people to full righteousness.

▶ **God's anger** has consequences. If people fail to turn from wrongdoing, God's anger can bring about death, exile, or even the destruction of a nation.

Reading the Bible, I encountered not a misty vapor but an actual Person. A Person as unique and distinctive and colorful as any person I know. God has deep emotions; he feels delight and frustration and anger.

Philip Yancey

27

question

▼

Does God get tired and need a rest or vacation?

On the Tour de France bicyclists toil up mountainsides, freewheel down steep descents, and race through crowded towns along the way. The Tour de France is run in stages because the racers need rest times along the grueling, tiresome route to rebuild their strength. According to the Bible, God's work is never-ending. He does not work in stages or start something and stop in the middle. So does God ever get tired and need a rest?

answer

▼

The Bible assures readers that the powerful, only true God never rests. Only created beings like people and animals need the restorative powers of sleep. God is not a created being so He does not get tired or weary. Isaiah says God is a wakeful, watchful keeper of His children, always attentive, always on duty.

God never gets tired, either. Isaiah contrasts God with a common blacksmith. The blacksmith forges iron and pounds it into shape with repeated hammer blows. But as he works, he gets hungry and thirsty. He loses his strength and gets tired. Isaiah says that, like the blacksmith, God, the master Potter, uses His tools to work His clay. He makes His pots and remakes them into what He wants them to be. But unlike the blacksmith, God never gets hungry, thirsty, or tired. God continues His work without ceasing, without even an inclination to nap.

God upholds the whole creation and governs all the creatures and does so without a rest. Because He never grows weary, God stands at the ready to come to the aid of His children. Because God never needs a holiday, His ear is always attentive to those who call on His name. Because He never leaves His post to someone else so that He can rest or relax, God is always in control of the events of history. What comfort there is in knowing God is available. He never sleeps, never rests, and never takes a vacation.

worth thinking about

▶ **God's power** is never exhausted because God never tires. That means He is always powerfully in control of everything that concerns you.

▶ **The psalmist** assured readers that God does not even take a nap. As He watches over you, His eyes neither droop nor blur. He neither slumbers nor sleeps.

▶ **Because God never** sleeps, there is no need to worry about anything. He is awake, so let Him take care of all the things that could possibly go wrong.

> *Do you not know? Have you not heard? The LORD is the everlasting God, the Creator of the ends of the earth. He will not grow tired or weary, and his understanding no one can fathom.*
>
> Isaiah 40:28, NIV

question

Does God hate anyone or anything?

Day and night. Good and bad. Love and hate. Each pair reflects a contradictory state or an opposite. Opposites can attract. A magnet's positive pole will be attracted to its negative pole. But most often opposites do not coexist. Day and night may blend at twilight, but no one would ever confuse daytime with nighttime. Because the Bible says God's nature is love, can love's opposite be a part of God's nature, too? Can God hate anyone or anything?

answer

Hate is compatible with God's nature in one way. Because God is holy and perfect, God can by no means tolerate wrongdoing. Therefore, the Bible says God hates sin and wickedness. But Proverbs suggests there are several other sins that God expressly hates. These sins are most distasteful to God because they hurt not only the one doing them, but other people, too.

According to Proverbs, God hates any form of pride or arrogance. When people overvalue themselves and undervalue others, this is especially hateful to God. He values all persons equally. God also hates a lying tongue, for God is truth. Nothing is more needed in conversation than truth at all times.

God also considers hands that kill innocent people, minds that devise wicked plans, and feet that rush quickly to do wickedness as hateful sins. Persons with wicked hands, minds, and feet will feel God's hate.

God also hates the giving of false testimony. This sin greatly disrespects God and injures others. But God saves His worst hate for those who are family troublemakers. Those who slander, tell ill-natured stories, spread jealousies, or stir up conflict among relatives are working at cross-purposes to God's love, peace, patience, gentleness, kindness, goodness, and self-control. Be careful not to commit one of God's hated sins.

worth thinking about

▶ **Moses said God** hated the practice of giving a sacrifice that was flawed in any way. God wants people to give the best they have back to Him.

▶ **Solomon reminded** readers that God hates every thought of those who are wicked but that He is pleased by the thoughts of those who are pure in heart.

▶ **The prophet Zechariah** wrote that God hates any plotting against your neighbor or swearing falsely about anything whether in thought, word, or deed.

Here are six things GOD hates, and one more that he loathes with a passion: eyes that are arrogant, a tongue that lies, hands that murder the innocent, a heart that hatches evil plots, feet that race down a wicked track, a mouth that lies under oath, a troublemaker in the family.

Proverbs 6:16–19, THE MESSAGE

29 question

What does God do all day?

Some companies sponsor a Bring Your Child to Work Day so that children have a better understanding of what parents do on the job. After one such day, a child was asked to share what he had learned about his father's job. With a stifled yawn the boy replied, "All he does is meet." Sometimes it appears to people that all God does is answer prayer. But is that true? What really does God do all day?

answer

While the Bible says that God is always attentive to the voice of His children, God does a lot more than just listen to and answer prayers. Part of what God does all day is work in cooperation with people's work. According to Psalms, human labor is futile unless God puts it into process. Exodus reveals God is the One who gives people the abilities they need to do work. Paul reminded the Corinthians that their generosity was linked to God's work of giving to them. Genesis says people cultivate what God already has created. And Hosea and Jeremiah declared the prophets wrote and spoke only what God had spoken to them.

God works in this world, too. According to the Book of Isaiah, God actively rules over the nations, calling up different ones to places of importance while reducing others to subservience or annihilation. God has also been at work in the nation of Israel. He called Abraham to a land God promised would be his. God set apart his descendants, gave them victory in battle, delivered them from slavery in Egypt, and raised up leaders to solidify them as the nation of Israel. God still watches over Israel, working out His promise to bring them into a land of peace and prosperity.

And God is at work every day in human life, too. He intervenes, guides, guards, and directs the lives of His children. His daily work can be seen through you.

worth thinking about

▶ **Because God is** at work in individual's lives, the psalmist says people should acknowledge their dependence on God and be grateful for His help.

▶ **God is actively** at work in creation. The Bible says God sustains the created order of the plants and animals, the stars and planets, and all other living things.

▶ **God also works** in the church. As a head directs the movement of a body, so God acts as the head of His church to direct its growth and ministry.

> *Jesus answered them, "My Father is always working, and I too must work."*
> John 5:17, GNT

question

▼

Does God have a plan for this planet?

In a computer simulation game, individuals allocate areas of land for different purposes. Parks, neighborhoods, shopping centers, schools, hospitals, and industrial areas are placed by a gamer in an attempt to make this simulated cityscape an inviting environment for its residents. In the real world developers do the same thing, scoping out properties and planning the use areas for whole counties. But what about a worldwide use plan or strategy? Does God have a plan for this planet?

answer

▼

When God formed the earth into dry land and seas, He was beginning to put into place His strategy for this world, because the Bible says God does indeed have a plan for planet Earth. As you search the pages of scripture, you can piece together that plan. Genesis says God intended this world to be a perfect place—no thorns or briars, no drought or disastrous weather patterns, no pests or pestilence. But the wrongdoing of humanity has delayed that plan of God's. However, Revelation says at the end of time God will remake the earth just as perfect as it was on the first day the sun shone across its waters.

But God's plan for the planet does not stop with the land and seas. God is concerned about everything He created. His ultimate plan for the earth also touches humanity. Daniel says that for centuries God has been setting up rulers of nations to work out His plan within those nations. And just as land developers set up use areas, the Book of Acts says God sets the borders of the nations and determines the lengths of times that rulers will rule. God also determines the exact places where people will live.

Yet God's plan for this planet goes even deeper. The prophet Jeremiah said God wants a personal relationship with individuals, from the least to the greatest. God wants you to know Him. That is part of His plan for this planet, too.

worth thinking about

▶ Because God determines the places people will live, that means God knows your address. It is part of His plan for this planet.

▶ According to Isaiah, God's plan for the earth includes a time of praise and worship. The earth and its inhabitants should sing and cry out for God's glory.

▶ The Bible says God created the earth to be His possession and show everyone His handiwork. His plan is to use the world He made for His honor and glory.

> *In spite of all appearances to the contrary, God still has a plan for this bankrupt world. . . .*
> *This earth of ours, He still wants as a theatre for His grace and glorious direction.*
> Helmut Thielicke

31 question

▼

What does God expect from people?

When you see a firefighter running into a burning building, you expect him to rescue people and put out the fire. When you see the mail carrier coming your way, you expect to be handed some mail. When you see a friend walking down the sidewalk, you expect her to stop and say hello. People live with expectations about how other people will behave. But if God met you on the sidewalk, what would He expect from you?

answer

▼

In an older Bible teaching tool used by many churches, students learn questions and answers about God and the Bible. The first lesson in this catechism echoes the question on this page as it asks, "What is the chief end of man?" The textbook response—to glorify God and enjoy Him forever—states one of God's expectations of people as revealed in Deuteronomy. This book of the Law says God expects His children to glorify Him by being faithful and obedient to Him.

Obedience requires God's children to live a certain way. The Book of Leviticus stresses God's expectation that His children will show love for one another as they live in community together. Proverbs says God expects honesty and truth in word and deed. The prophet Amos declared God's expectation for justice and righteousness in all dealings between people. Paul urged Timothy's church to strive for God's expectation of unity and peace. Peter reminded his readers that God expects His children to live by higher moral standards than the rest of the world.

The Bible says God also expects His children to be thankful, to give Him praise and worship, and to strive for holiness in everything they do, say, or think. Children are expected to honor their parents. Parents are expected to raise their children to know God. Spouses are expected to love each other. And bosses are expected to be just and kind. Ultimately God's expectation of people is for each one to be just like Him.

worth thinking about

▶ **God expects** His children to follow His will as set out in the Law and the Prophets. To fulfill this expectation God's children need to pray and study the Bible.

▶ **In Matthew's Gospel,** Jesus said God expected two things from people: to love God with all your heart, soul, and mind and to love your neighbor as yourself.

▶ **According to the Gospels,** God will reward those who fulfill God's expectation of obedience.

> *He's already made it plain how to live, what to do, what GOD is looking for in men and women. It's quite simple: Do what is fair and just to your neighbor, be compassionate and loyal in your love, and don't take yourself too seriously—take God seriously.*
>
> Micah 6:8, THE MESSAGE

32

question

What is God's purpose for angels?

Renaissance artists often chose stories from the Bible as the backdrop for their paintings and frescoes. Whether detailing the expulsion of Adam and Eve from the Garden of Eden, the crucifixion and burial of Christ, or a nativity scene of the Madonna and Child, almost every artist included at least one angel. These celestial beings seemed to oversee the major events of human history. But was that assumption about angels accurate? How do angels really fit into God's purpose?

answer

According to the Bible, angels are spiritual beings who act as God's servants with specific, though limited, responsibilities. Sometimes God will send angels to serve as His deliverers. When the Assyrians besieged King Hezekiah, 2 Kings says God sent His angels to scatter the enemy and deliver Jerusalem. When Peter was imprisoned for preaching about Jesus, the Book of Acts says God sent an angel who woke Peter and freed him from his cell.

The Bible also says angels attend to the needs of God's people, but only when God sends them. An angel, carrying bread and water, was dispatched to help Elijah as he slept under a broom tree. Angels were sent to Abraham to warn him of the impending destruction of Sodom and Gomorrah. Angels were then sent to take Lot and his family forcibly by the hand to pull them to safety. Luke records an angel's visit to strengthen Jesus on the night He prayed in the Garden of Gethsemane.

Angels also act as God's representatives. When Stephen stood before the council in Jerusalem, he reminded the Jewish leaders that the law given on Mount Sinai was received through the hands of God's angels. Job says angels wait for God to summon them should they be needed as God's intermediaries at death. And Revelation declares at the end of time, God's angels will be sent once again as His representatives to proclaim Jesus Christ's return to earth and God's final judgment of the world.

worth thinking about

▶ **The Bible says** angels serve as messengers, bringing God's words to people. For example, God sent His angels to tell Joseph and the shepherds about Christ's birth.

▶ **Several named angels** in the Bible had specific duties. The Book of Daniel says that Michael, the archangel, has the job of protecting the nation of Israel.

▶ **Angels sometimes appear** to human beings. God's angels appeared to Isaiah, Daniel, and Zechariah to bring them a message of hope in the midst of coming destruction.

> *The function of God's angels is to execute the plan of divine providence, even in earthly things.*
> Saint Thomas Aquinas

33

▼

Does God help only those who help themselves?

America has been called the Land of Opportunity. Supposedly there are enough resources and career paths available for individuals to better themselves. In American history, rags-to-riches stories abound. Each tale suggests people succeeded through their own hard work and determination. Only occasionally would anyone receive a helping hand. But is this God's way? Do people have to go it alone to succeed in faith and life? Does God help only those who help themselves?

answer

▼

Some have suggested God will only come alongside and help you grow in your faith and life if you take the first step and work on bettering yourself on your own. Unfortunately, this "bootstrap theology"—pulling yourself up to a better place by your own hard work—is not a biblical principle. Instead God willingly helps anyone who asks, not just those who help themselves.

There are times when the Bible indicates God does help those who are living life God's way. The psalmist sang God's praises for doing what was right as He helped those who also were doing right. Isaiah echoed this theme, recognizing God's helpful activity in the lives of those who enjoy doing good and living the way God wants them to live. Ezra, too, spoke of God's help directed toward everyone who obeyed God's commands.

Yet the Bible also says God sometimes waits to help until someone asks. The Bible says if people ask, God's wisdom is available to those who need help. But Isaiah rejoiced that God came to his aid unsummoned, noting twice in one chapter that God helped him learn and also helped him stand firm so he wouldn't be ashamed in his faith.

God truly helps those who seek His help, not just those who help themselves. You do not have to work until you are worn out for God to come to your aid. The Bible says God's help is only a prayer away.

worth thinking about

▶ **Your salvation** is in no way a product of your own hard work. Instead it is a gift of God's grace that is accepted by faith.

▶ **You do not have** to help yourself when faced with temptation. Jesus, God's Son, suffered temptation but did not give in. You can pray and ask for His help when tempted.

▶ **The Bible says** God actually seeks to help those who cannot help themselves—folks like the poor, the sick, the widowed, and the orphaned.

> *Really! There's no such thing as self-rescue, pulling yourself up by your bootstraps. The cost of rescue is beyond our means.*
> Psalm 49:7–8, THE MESSAGE

34

Why did God send Jesus to the world?

Why do giraffes have such long necks? Why do clouds hold rain? Why do people have two eyes but only one mouth? People want to know the "why" about things to help put the bits and pieces in perspective. Knowing why helps connect the dots of seemingly unconnected or unrelated events. So what is the connection between Jesus' life here on earth and God's involvement in everything? Why did God send Jesus to the world in the first place?

answer

Throughout the Bible, readers are reminded that God is holy and people are not. For people to enjoy God's presence and live with God in heaven, the playing field needs to be leveled. People need to be holy like God is holy. But people are not naturally saintly. Little things can set tempers flaring and can cause someone to say hurtful words or think spiteful thoughts. The Bible says everyone has done something wrong at some time in life. Because of this, everyone needs an inner change of heart.

The Gospel of John records a conversation between Jesus and a teacher of the Jewish law named Nicodemus who sought an inner change of heart. Jesus reminded Nicodemus that God's law required a payment of a life, a spilling of blood, for every wrongdoing. Jesus said He came as God's Son to earth for the express purpose of shedding His blood to pay for humanity's wickedness. Every person who believes that Jesus died to pay the penalty for his or her personal mistakes and wrongdoing will receive the inner change of heart that the Bible calls salvation. Salvation will guarantee each person everlasting life in heaven with God.

Though the Bible says a lot about Jesus' role as the final Judge of the world, the Bible also says God did not send His Son, Jesus, to the world to condemn the world for wickedness and wrongdoing. God loved people so much He sent Jesus to be a payment, a heart changer, a Savior.

worth thinking about

▶ The motivation for God sending Jesus to the world was pure love. The motivation for Jesus' dying on the cross was pure obedience.

▶ John's Gospel says Jesus did not have to come to the world to condemn it. The world has been condemned since Adam and Eve disobeyed God.

▶ The Bible says Jesus' first coming to earth was as a Savior, but He will come again to earth as King of kings and Lord of lords.

> *The modern intelligent mind . . . has got to be shocked afresh by the audacious central Fact—that as a sober matter of history God became One of us.*
>
> J. B. Phillips

35 question

Does God bless some people and curse others?

There are people in every community who seem to have life easy. They possess comfortable homes and fancy cars. They enjoy lavish lifestyles. Their investments produce increasing income. Such folks seem to be blessed. But then there are others who have no job, no money, and no prospects. Every day is full of bad breaks and trouble. With the vast difference between the two types of people, one might wonder, does God bless some people and curse others?

answer

Because God is love, He blesses. At creation, God blessed Adam and Eve with the ability to bear children and with the job of exercising authority over the earth. When God spoke to Abraham, He promised to bless him and bless the world through Abraham's descendants. When God chose the nation of Israel to be His people, He promised to bless them with good health and long life, with lots of children and livestock and with a peaceful homeland. To bless people with spiritual and material benefits is a part of God's nature, and He is the source of all blessing in the world whether people realize it or not.

But bad things happen in this world, too. Curses befall nations and individuals. Why? Because of Adam and Eve. When Eve chose to disobey God and eat the forbidden fruit, God's hand of perfect blessing was removed from the earth. Genesis says that the ground was cursed because of Eve's wrongdoing and that the snake was cursed because of its role in Eve's deception. When Eve chose to disobey God, her wrongdoing opened the door to all the curses and misfortune that have taken place on the earth ever since.

However, the Bible does say God will bless some folks and allow misfortune to happen to others. The Bible bears witness to both occurrences. Yet curses can become blessings if they help turn hearts back to God. Whether God sends blessings or allows misfortune, He is still God and worthy of praise.

worth thinking about

- ▶ **Obedience plays** a part in receiving God's blessing. God often issued "if/then" promises—if you do what He says, then He will bless you in a certain way.

- ▶ **Perspective can put** a fresh spin on whether something is a blessing or a curse. A one-room efficiency could be a mansion to a wartime refugee.

- ▶ **Because God** is good and can do no evil, He is not the source of curses. Satan is. Disobedience to God's ways opens the door for Satan's misfortunes.

God particularly pours out his blessings upon those who know how much they need him.
Robert H. Schuller

What does God do all day?

You have bedded me down in lush meadows, you find me quiet pools to drink from. True to your word, you let me catch my breath and send me in the right direction.

Psalm 23:2–3, The Message

question

Does God expect people to respond when He speaks?

In a workplace chain of command, the boss may ask an assistant for a report for an upcoming meeting. Depending on everyone's schedule, the job may finally fall to someone four tiers below the assistant, but the report will be completed and bubbled back up to the boss. Unfortunately, folks sometimes follow the same procedure when it comes to God. God speaks, but they pass His words down the line. They do not own the responsibility of follow-through. But should they?

answer

According to the Bible, people do have a responsibility to do what God says. The Bible labels this responsibility "obedience" and provides extensive examples of people who accepted the responsibility of following God's words. Genesis records the obedience of Noah to build the ark and of Joseph to serve Potiphar. Numbers shows the Levites responding to God's words and becoming the priests of Israel. Ezekiel took on the responsibility God gave him to be a watchman on the wall.

Yet God sometimes allows a delegation of responsibility. David obeyed God's words in 1 Chronicles and stepped aside to let Solomon build the temple for the Lord. In

Exodus, Moses did as God said and chose leaders to help him judge God's people. And in the Book of Acts, the early church leaders harkened to God's direction and delegated the responsibility for feeding the widows to seven reliable men.

What God does not allow, however, is a denial or shirking of responsibility. When people evade responsibility, trouble and punishment follow. In Genesis, Adam and Eve ate the fruit God said they were not to touch. Their disobedience led to their expulsion from the Garden of Eden and ultimate death. In 1 Samuel, Saul did not do what God said and did not destroy everything that belonged to the Amalekites. Though Saul blamed others for the situation, his shirking of responsibility led to his removal as king of Israel. These people forgot that when God speaks, He expects His people to obey.

worth thinking about

▶ **In Genesis,** God gave people the responsibility for the keeping of His world and for exercising control over the animal kingdom.

▶ **According to the** Book of Romans, God has given national leaders the responsibility to administer justice, reward good, and punish wrongdoing.

▶ **God has given** a responsibility to all of His children to love Him and be His representative to those who do not know Jesus Christ.

> *All the people responded together, "We will do all that the LORD has spoken."*
>
> Exodus 19:8, HCSB

37 question

Does God expect people to do hard things or live hard lives?

Three Hebrew teenagers found themselves in a foreign land. The king of the realm demanded their worship of a golden statue whenever the harps and horns played. Because the teens revered God, they refused the king's order and found themselves thrown into a furnace heated seven times hotter than normal. Did God expect these teens to make this tough choice? To live in such hard circumstances? To face such hard times? Does God expect that of people today, too?

answer

Suffering happens in life because of wrongdoing. The Bible says the tables were turned from a life of justice and peace to a life of injustice and strife when the first man and woman disobeyed God. Now those who hurt, steal from, and kill others often prosper while the innocent, caring, and good often find themselves facing hard times. While God does not expect people to experience hard times, the Bible is realistic about suffering in this world. Suffering happens. Yet because God is with them, His children are able to bear tough times with dignity and hope.

In tough times God is sometimes the closest to His children. The Book of Daniel says God protected the three

Hebrew teenagers and sent His Son to be in the furnace with them. When they were released from the furnace, only their ropes had burned away. Their clothes were untouched and did not even smell like fire. When Paul and Silas were jailed for delivering a slave girl from demons, the Book of Acts says God intervened for them and sent an earthquake that freed them from their shackles. And in Genesis, when Hagar and her child were dying of thirst in the desert, God found her and directed her to a nearby well.

While God may not expect people to do hard things or live hard lives, bad things will happen. But God is greater than those hard times. He promises to be with His children in every circumstance.

worth thinking about

▶ For those who do not trust God, hard times and suffering can bring about a hardness of heart toward God and His ways.

▶ The causes of suffering are varied—human cruelty, aging, family troubles, Satan's activity, etc. In all these situations, God stands ready to help and deliver.

▶ Because God is loving and shows concern for those who suffer, blaming God for hard times is just as wrong as patting yourself on the back when things go well.

When you go through deep waters, I will be with you. When you go through rivers of difficulty, you will not drown. When you walk through the fire of oppression, you will not be burned up; the flames will not consume you. For I am the LORD, your God.

Isaiah 43:2–3, NLT

38

Does God save people because of the good things they do?

In many businesses, employees are rewarded for good performance with merit raises or bonus checks. In schools and universities, students who consistently do well are often the recipients of scholarships, awards, or other forms of recognition. Communities also bestow honors on those citizens who are charitable and do good things for others in their neighborhood. But is God impressed with these good deeds? Will God save people and let them into heaven because of the good things they do?

answer

You might have heard people say they were sure God would let them into heaven because they are basically good people. They have not murdered anyone. They live respectable lives and try to do good things and help others whenever they can. Surely, they say, this would be enough to get them through the pearly gates of heaven.

Indeed, doing good deeds is encouraged in the Bible. In his letter to the Ephesians, Paul reminded his readers that God creates all people and it is God's plan that people do good things for one another. Paul said God has prepared these good works ahead of time so that if people are paying attention and doing what God wants they will see the opportunities for good deeds all along the path of life.

But Paul also added a qualification to this message, reminding his readers that salvation—the work that God performs in a human heart to prepare it for heaven—is a gift from God. No one can earn salvation and heaven through good works, charitable deeds, or any self-oriented sacrifice. If you could earn salvation and get to heaven through good works, Paul said, you would have huge bragging rights. But this is not God's way. Paul said salvation comes only through faith in God's gracious gift of forgiveness provided through the sacrificial death of His Son, Jesus. The Bible says good works are good to do, but they are not enough to save your soul.

worth thinking about

▶ The Old Testament prophet Isaiah said that in God's eyes, all the good deeds and righteous acts of people are like dirty, stinking rags.

▶ Because God has created you to do good works, you will be happier doing good works than not doing them.

▶ Salvation comes when a heart is remade in God's likeness by God's power. Good works are neither needed nor useful for this work of God's grace.

> We are not saved "by works," by anything we did or can do. It was all God's work of grace in us, so we have no reason to boast, no grounds for feeling a sense of accomplishment.
> James Montgomery Boice

39 question

What is God's purpose behind heaven and hell?

In C. S. Lewis's book *The Great Divorce*, passengers on a bus find themselves in a great, darkened city. In this hellish atmosphere, people are suspicious, distancing themselves from one another. Some are tormented by voices; others frightened by the dark; others wander the streets in confusion. It is a pointless place. Yet the Bible says God is a purposeful God. He is never pointless in His actions. So does God have a purpose behind heaven and hell?

answer

In Matthew's Gospel, Jesus told several parables about the final judgment. He said every person will be sentenced to either everlasting happiness or never-ending misery. When He, the Son of man, returns to earth, people will be divided into two groups. Those who have done what God wants will be ushered into the blessedness of heaven. However, those who have been unjust, ungodly, or have failed to follow God's way will find themselves cursed and sent into the eternal fires of hell that are "prepared for the Devil and his angels" (Matthew 25:41, HCSB).

But why would God do this? Why would God set up two different places for judgment like heaven and hell? The answer is tied to God's nature. Because God is holy, people also must be holy if they want to be in His presence. God cannot coexist with evil. So God set up two different places to send judged humanity. Only the righteous will live with God in heaven; the unholy will go to hell. Unfortunately, the Bible says all people are unrighteous, no matter how good they seem. So all people are doomed to live apart from God in hell.

Yet God loves people, so He offers a way out of hell. Paul said, "God made Christ, who never sinned, to be the offering for our sin, so that we could be made right with God" (2 Corinthians 5:21, NLT). By becoming right with God, people can enjoy perfect fellowship with Him forever in heaven.

worth thinking about

▶ *Sheol*, the place of the dead, is the Old Testament word for "hell." In the New Testament, *Gehenna* is its equivalent and means "the place of the wicked."

▶ Jesus said the thief on the cross would be with Him in *paradise*. This Persian term was used by the Jews to denote the destination of the righteous after death.

▶ According to the Bible, heaven is a place of continual worship and service to God. Hell, on the other hand, is completely separated from God's light, love, and peace.

> *The way to hell's a seeming heaven.*
> Frances Quarles

40

What does God promise to those who follow His will and way?

An advertising circular for a furniture company promises a night of unbroken sleep if you purchase their mattress set. A television ad promises stronger muscles and less weight if you use their exercise machine. A can of soup promises to warm icy children if you serve the soup hot from the stove. People are bombarded by companies who promise guaranteed results if folks follow their directions. So what does God promise to those who follow His directions, will, and way?

answer

God promises weightier results than a good night's sleep, stronger muscles, or a warmed body to those who follow His will. In fact, the Bible says God's promises to His followers are never-ending. Luke says God's followers will receive the gift of the Holy Spirit—both now and for eternity. John says those who follow God's will are granted full forgiveness, a promised resurrection, and an eternal life with God in heaven at the end of time. Isaiah proclaims an everlasting sense of God's presence for those who follow His ways. Jeremiah declares a never-ending knowledge of God for His followers, and the psalmist promises endless joy to all who keep God's will and way.

The Bible also says God will provide for those who follow His will. God will give guidance, healing, wisdom, and material provision. He will ensure forgiveness, salvation, and victory over temptation. The apostle Paul rejoiced that God promised lasting peace to those who follow His will. God also promises protection and a perfect plan for each individual life that is committed to following His way. But best of all, John promised that those who followed God's will and way would become God's children. Their prayers would always find their way to God's throne, and Jesus would be their big brother.

God's presence and provision. His plan and protection. His forgiveness and promise of family. Weighty promises all; and all are guaranteed to those who follow God's will and way.

worth thinking about

▶ God promises His unceasing presence to those who follow His will and way. God will never abandon you.

▶ To those who follow God's will and way, God's promises stand ready. They are given and spoken, but because some are not dated, like the promise of Jesus' return to earth, only God knows when they will be fulfilled.

▶ God promises His followers access to the throne of heaven through every prayer. Spending time with God this way will guarantee true beauty of life and character.

> *To all who believed him and accepted him, he gave the right to become children of God.*
> John 1:12, NLT

question

Has God ever made any mistakes?

People usually define a mistake as an error, committed either through a lack of skill or knowledge or attention to detail. Calling a wrong number, for example, might be such a mistake. Another type of mistake may be a misunderstanding or misconception or possibly a slipup in the evaluation or interpretation of facts, such as mistaking someone for someone else. Because people are prone to such blunders, one might ask if God ever had any reason to say, "Oops! I made a mistake."

answer

According to the Bible, when Job's life fell apart, three friends came to offer him some comfort. Their words, however, were not very consoling. Those friends believed Job's misfortune was a judgment of God for some wrong Job must have committed. Upset at their assessment, Job declared his innocence, claiming it was God who had made the mistake. Yet by reading the Bible story, one can ultimately see that God made no mistake in Job's life, nor was He punishing Job for a wrongdoing.

People often view circumstances and situations from the limited perspective of personal experience. When God is examined this way, it can appear that He makes mistakes.

But as in the case of Job, appearances can be deceiving. Instead of evaluating God's performance based on personal experience, circumstance, or situation, a better tool is needed. That tool is the Bible.

Scripture repeatedly declares God's faultlessness. He is complete in every way, not lacking in any skill or knowledge. The psalmist proclaimed God is ethically perfect, doing nothing out of spite. Isaiah announced God's perfect faithfulness, a keeper of promises from the beginning of time. Jeremiah stated that every aspect of everything God does is perfect. His attention to detail is flawless. The apostle Paul asserted that God, in the person of His Son, Jesus, lived a perfect life here on earth and that God's will and ways are also perfect. Rest assured, almighty God does not make mistakes—whether in the past, present, or future.

worth thinking about

▶ Because God does not make mistakes, nothing He plans or sets into motion can be changed, including His plan for your life.

▶ Any assessment of a personal circumstance that seems to indicate God made a mistake will be proven wrong if reevaluated in light of the Bible.

▶ God's perfection is a concept people find incomprehensible yet comforting at the same time. Just check out Job's story.

> *God is too wise to ever make a mistake*
> *and too loving to ever be unkind.*
> Duane Pederson

42 question

Can God be trusted?

A small child perches on the edge of a swimming pool. An older relative urges the child to jump into the water by promising, "Jump in! I'll catch you!" The child will not jump if that child believes the older family member cannot be trusted to fulfill their claim. Reliance on someone is essential to trust. So, if you are standing on the edge of a disaster or decision, can God be trusted to come through for you?

answer

The Bible assures you of the total trustworthiness of God. The psalmist and the prophet Jeremiah stressed the honesty of God compared to the dishonesty of the world. God's honesty makes Him trustworthy. The Book of Exodus contends that God is trustworthy because He is not corruptible. He is not influenced by greed or self-promotion. Proverbs reminds readers that God's trustworthiness is proven by His ability to keep confidences, and the Gospels state God's faithfulness in His dealings with people proves you can trust Him. Indeed, the prophet Zechariah declared God's trustworthiness because He is truthful in all His words and deeds.

Scripture also indicates there are positive results to be found in trusting God. When you trust God with your life and seek to live according to His purpose, Isaiah says you will experience peace. When you trust God and let that trust grow by getting to know God better through Bible study and daily communication in prayer, the psalmist said, you will be freed from fear and will experience lasting joy. Proverbs says God will bless you materially for your trust; Isaiah says you will find strength for each day when you trust God; and Jeremiah says your physical body will see lasting benefits from trusting Him, too.

So can God be trusted to come through for you? You bet! You can jump into life with the full assurance that God has set aside His best for His children. Now that is something to praise God for!

worth thinking about

- ▶ **Forsaking God** and placing your trust in other people, in wealth, or in your own strength is pointless and provokes God's anger.

- ▶ **Because God can** be trusted, His children are to be trustworthy, too—in relationships, in faith, at work, and at home.

- ▶ **According to the psalmist,** God's words as revealed in the Bible are completely true, dependable, and able to be trusted, too.

> *Some trust in chariots and some in horses,*
> *but we trust in the name of the LORD our God.*
> Psalm 20:7, NIV

43 question

How does God adapt to stay current with the times?

If you were to compare a home built in the 1880s with a home built in the last twenty years, you would find major construction differences. Builders have to adapt over time to available materials, construction codes, and personal preferences. Time forces change. Manufacturers gear up for new products. Banks offer new services. Schools teach new curricula. Change helps people stay current with what is going on in society. But how does God adapt to stay current with the times?

answer

God is the master of time. Therefore, God is not affected by time as people are. He does not need to flex or change with the seasons or alterations in societies. In fact, one of the facets of God's character is His unchangeableness. The Bible says God's personality, plans, and procedures do not change with time. Though He maintains active, vital, and growing relationships with individuals, God's being is unchanged and unchangeable. He does not need to adapt to stay current with time because God is the source of all time. God is constant. People are the ones who change.

The writer of Hebrews praised God for this unchangeableness. Though people change like a garment, God remains the same—yesterday, today, and forever. Malachi voiced this principle centuries before as he quoted God saying, "I am GOD—yes, I AM. I haven't changed" (Malachi 3:6, THE MESSAGE).

It is true. God does not need to change anything to stay current with the times. His message of forgiveness is as applicable today as it was when Abraham walked the earth. His promises are as sure to be fulfilled today as when He gave His first promise to Adam. His love is as constant today as it was before He created the world. And His purposes and plans, His will and way, have not changed since He hung the stars in the night sky and gave them their names. God is unchangeable. He is the only sure, solid hope for a constantly changing world.

worth thinking about

▶ **Governments revise** social policies with laws and judicial renderings. But God has no need to revise His law or judgments. The Bible says God's laws are eternal.

▶ **Because God** does not change to fit the times, the psalmist assured readers that God's love, promises, and kingdom will continue eternally.

▶ **God's Word,** the Bible, reflects God's unchangeableness. God said His Word would stand forever; no one could add or subtract from His words.

> *Every good and perfect gift is from above, coming down from the Father of the heavenly lights, who does not change like shifting shadows.*
> James 1:17, NIV

question

Does God keep His promises?

Sign a note with a bank, and you have made a promise to pay back a loan. Call a doctor for a checkup, and you have made a promise to keep an appointment. Stand up before a judge or preacher at your wedding, and you have made a promise for better or worse. Unfortunately, the promises people make sometimes get broken. Marriages dissolve; loans default; and doctor's appointments are missed by accident. But what about God? Does He keep His promises?

answer

The Bible says unequivocally that God is a promise keeper. In the Old Testament, God made many commitments to Abraham, promising him a son when Abraham was already a senior citizen, guaranteeing him more heirs than there were stars in the sky, and pledging to give Abraham and his heirs all the land Abraham could see. These commitments might have seemed far-fetched and impossible, but over the centuries God has kept every promise He made to Abraham.

Yet God's promises did not stop with Abraham. He made promises to the ancient Israelites, too. Just before Moses died, he reminded the Israelites that none of the promises

God ever made to them were left unfulfilled. Every promise was kept. No pledge, commitment, or guarantee was lacking.

The New Testament writers reminded readers of God's fulfilled promises, too. Jesus promised to send the Holy Spirit so that God's presence could be with people forever. According to the Book of Acts, that promise was fulfilled during the early days of Christianity. The Book of Hebrews reminded people to hold firmly to the hope they had in God. God can be trusted to keep His promise no matter what, the writer of Hebrews declared.

Truly, you can trust God to keep every promise He makes, whether in the past, present, or future.

worth thinking about

▶ **Some of God's** promises are future-based: Jesus' return to earth, the final judgment of the world, and the revealing of a home in heaven for God's children.

▶ **Because God keeps** his promises, His children should follow His example and keep their promises, too.

▶ **God has made** some promises that do not harbor good things, like promises of judgment for wrongdoing. Because God is a promise keeper, He will keep those promises, too.

> *Let us hold tightly without wavering to the hope we affirm, for God can be trusted to keep his promise.*
> Hebrews 10:23, NLT

45

question

What did God promise He would never do again?

Recovering alcoholics rarely say they will never take another drink. Rather, they keep their resolve to a one-day-at-a-time philosophy, pledging to refrain from drink for this one day or this one hour. Because people are not very good at keeping short-term promises, recovering alcoholics know a promise to never do something could be an exercise in futility. Yet God is good at keeping all His promises—even the "never again" ones. So what did God promise He would never do again?

answer

God made several "never again" promises in the Bible—three within the first ten chapters of Genesis alone. In the story of the Flood, God destroyed every living thing on earth except for the animals He preserved with Noah and his family in the ark. When Noah emerged from the ark and built an altar of thanksgiving to God, God promised Himself to never again curse the ground and destroy every living thing because of the wickedness of people. People have continued to do wicked things, but God has kept His promise.

Yet God was not finished with His "never again" promises. God promised Noah that He would never again flood the earth. The rainbow was God's sign to humanity that He would keep His promise. In addition, God spoke directly to the ancient Israelites in the Sinai wilderness and promised to never break His covenant with them, reminding them He had already fulfilled His promises to deliver them from Egypt and to bring them into the Promised Land.

When the Jews returned to their homeland after their seventy-year exile in Babylon, they were assured of two more "never again" promises. Isaiah proclaimed God had sworn to never again give Israel's grain as food to their enemies, and Jeremiah declared God would make an everlasting covenant with the children of Israel to never again stop doing them good. One thing is certain: Because God is God, His "never again" promises will never fail.

worth thinking about

- ▶ God made "never" promises to individuals, too. God told Joshua, "As I was with Moses, so I will be with you; I will never leave you" (Joshua 1:5, NIV).

- ▶ God said He would never take His love away from David's son Solomon. Instead, Solomon would be God's son and God would be his father.

- ▶ Through the prophet Joel, God promised there will come a day when His people will never again be a cause for ridicule among the nations.

> My future is as bright as the promises of God.
> Adoniram Judson

Can God be trusted?

Those who trust in the LORD are as secure as Mount Zion; they will not be defeated but will endure forever.

Psalm 125:1, NLT

46

question

Are there clear signs of God's unchanging grace?

Watch the passing of the seasons on oak or maple trees, and you will see change. These trees lie dormant throughout winter. But as the warmth of spring courses through the tree trunks, buds swell and leaves begin to emerge. The full leaves spread shade for hot summer days. But autumn's frost colors the leaves, sending them falling to the ground. The trees change with the seasons. But does God change? Can you see clear signs of God's unchanging grace?-

answer

God's grace—His unearned favor and forbearance—is closely allied to His mercy. Both are aspects of God's personality through which He shows compassion, acceptance, and generosity to faulty, sinful human beings. God's grace is clearly evidenced throughout the Bible. In the Old Testament, God's grace saved Noah from the Flood and established an everlasting covenant with Abraham. God's grace corrected Jonah's direction and pardoned a repentant city that had been doomed to destruction. In the New Testament, God's grace healed the sick, fed the hungry, and blinded a man on his way to Damascus in order to send him as a messenger of God' grace to the world.

There are clear signs of God's grace at work today, too. Lamentations declares God's grace is seen anew every morning. Because of God's grace, the sun continues to shine and rain continues to fall. Because of God's grace, frail humanity receives His compassion. Because of God's grace, blessings still fall from God's hand. Hosea adds that because of God's grace, judgment is on hold. Humanity still lives, breathes, and experiences God's presence, all because of His grace.

In addition, God's unchanging grace is seen in His unchanging message of forgiveness and restoration. Paul reminded readers that "God has revealed his grace for the salvation of all people" (Titus 2:11, GNT). God graciously accepts all who ask and turn away from wrongdoing. It is by this unchanging grace that hearts can be made right, God's forgiveness can be applied, and eternal life can be secured.

worth thinking about

▶ **God's grace** never falters; 2 Thessalonians says people have a good hope.

▶ **God's unchanging grace** is always present with His people. If God withheld His grace and presence, humanity would have no recourse from sin or wrongdoing.

▶ **God's unchanging grace** is modeled in the prodigal son's father. Even when the son wasted everything, his father ran to him with outstretched arms of love.

> *Our gracious God not only leads us in the way of mercy, but he prepares our path before us, providing for all our wants even before they occur.*
> Charles H. Spurgeon

47

Has God ever changed His mind?

You go to the grocery store after work looking for something for supper. You pick up a rotisserie chicken sitting in the warmer by the deli counter. But then you glimpse a sign proclaiming SALE and see a mouthwatering delicacy you cannot resist. You change your mind, put the chicken back, and look forward to a scrumptious supper. People change their minds all the time. But has God ever changed His?

answer

It might appear in the Bible that God has changed His mind. For example, as Moses stood on Mount Sinai, God declared His intent to wipe out the idolatrous Israelites. Moses interceded for them, and God "changed His mind about the disaster He said He would bring on His people" (Exodus 32:14, HCSB). Again, in the Book of Amos, God was prepared to send locusts and fire on the latter harvest. Amos prayed for forgiveness and God relented. Jonah also said God changed His mind and refused to judge Nineveh when the people repented from their wrongdoing. So, did God really change His mind?

No. By nature God is changeless. According to the Book of Numbers, God is not like people. He cannot lie or change His mind. In fact, in every instance in the Bible where God relents from doing something, He is not changing His mind or plan. Rather, He is being consistent. He is doing what He said He would do from the very beginning. The Book of 2 Chronicles says if God's people humbled themselves and prayed and turned from wrongdoing, God would forgive. The prophet Isaiah said if a wicked person turns from wrongdoing and turns toward God, God will have mercy. And because God is gracious, compassionate, loving, and slow to anger, the prophet Joel said God will always turn away from sending calamity. God does not change His mind. People change theirs. And when people change their minds and follow God, He consistently keeps His word and changelessly forgives.

worth thinking about

▶ **Jeremiah said** King Hezekiah faced impending doom, but when Hezekiah tried to do what God wanted, Hezekiah's changed heart allowed God to relent from sending disaster.

▶ **Because God does not** change His mind, His plans are firmly set, and every promise He has given you in His Word will be kept.

▶ **God may not change** His mind, but He can change His judgments. Holds and stops have been put on judgments because prayers for forgiveness and mercy have been offered.

> *What peace it brings to the Christian's heart to realize that our heavenly Father never differs from himself. . . . Neither does he change his mind about anything.*
> A. W. Tozer

48 question
▼
Does God judge people?

According to legend, Santa Claus keeps a ledger to help him determine who has been naughty or nice through-out the year. A few days before Christmas, Mr. Claus will review his list and load his sleigh accordingly. Based on Santa's judgment, good children will receive toys, but bad children will find a lump of coal in their Christmas stockings. But does God keep a naughty-and-nice list throughout the year? Does God judge people, too?

answer

While God may not have an annual naughty-and-nice list, Revelation says He does keep a set of books to be used at the end of time to judge the world. All people, both the important and unimportant, will be called to stand before God's throne in heaven to be judged on how they lived their lives. According to the Book of Revelation, those who love God will be listed in God's Book of Life and will be rewarded with eternal life in heaven. However, people who are listed merely in God's book of the dead will find themselves living out an eternity of punishment. Peter added that God is withholding this final judgment so that all people might have the opportunity to change their ways, their judgment, and their final destiny.

The Bible also indicates that God judges people while they are still alive, too. Genesis says that after Cain murdered his brother God pronounced judgment on him, promising him an arduous life as a marked fugitive. According to 2 Chronicles, Elijah the prophet spoke God's judgment on a vile, wicked king of Israel, and King Jehoram lived the rest of his short life in misery and pain. Daniel records that Belshazzar, king of Babylon, incurred God's wrath when he used holy articles from God's temple for an all-night orgy. God judged him while the party raged. Invaders took Belshazzar's life and his throne.

So does God judge people? He does indeed.

worth thinking about

▶ **God warned Israel** that if the people did not keep His laws, He would judge them and remove His blessing. Twelve times in the Book of Judges, Israel received this sentence.

▶ **God will justly** judge ungodly nations. Obadiah tells of God's judgment on Edom; 1 Samuel records God's judgment on Assyria; and Isaiah recites God's judgment on Babylon.

▶ **The Bible says** God's judgments are always just. His timely judgment of people is meant to punish wrongdoing, vindicate the righteous, and turn people back to God.

> *The LORD sits enthroned forever; He has established His throne for judgment. He judges the world with righteousness.*
>
> Psalms 9:7–8, HCSB

question

Does God live by a set of rules?

Most states publish a driver's manual that discusses the rules to follow when operating a motor vehicle in that state. Included in the instructions are rules for approaching a four-way stop, which vehicle has the right of way in a traffic circle, and what you should do when emergency vehicles flash their lights. These rules of the road keep drivers, pedestrians, and property safe. Though God doesn't operate a motor vehicle, does He live by a set of rules?

answer

The Bible never speaks about a divine rule book because God is governed by rules that go beyond instruction books. God is ruled by His character. It is in God's nature to be loving, kind, just, faithful, forgiving, and true. He cannot be cruel, mean-spirited, unjust, unfaithful, vindictive, or false at any time for any reason. He is bound by His character to operate within His nature.

God also usually operates within the natural laws of the universe. He does not suspend the laws of gravity, thermodynamics, or physics to prove His sovereignty. He does not turn the grass from green to pink or purple to demonstrate His power over creation. And He does not ignore the frailty of the human body, but instead compassionately protects people by keeping the earth rotating around the sun so people do not freeze to death on an ice planet. Thus God lives by a set of rules that resonate within Himself and echo His love to all He has created.

Yet God also is ruled by His words. He cannot speak a prophecy through one of His servants saying something will happen and not bring it to pass. He cannot hang a rainbow in the sky and not remember His words about never sending another flood. He cannot promise to send blessings, bring lasting peace, or carry out a final judgment and not perform each word to the letter. What God promises, He will keep. God lives by this rule, too.

worth thinking about

- ▶ **God abides** by rules and expects people to do so, too. Keeping community laws and rules leads to peaceful coexistence. God wants His children to live at peace with others.

- ▶ **In the Bible**, God's set of rules are often referred to as covenants. In a covenant, God commits Himself to a specific requirement or action for a specified time.

- ▶ **The Ten Commandments** are God's written rules for His children to follow. These rules are important to God, and He promises to bless those who keep His commandments.

> *Just as God has equations and rules in the material realm, God has equations and rules in the spiritual.*
> Billy Graham

question

Is God fair in His dealings with people?

"That's not fair!" This accusation is often heard from adults at a union bargaining table when the offer is unacceptable. Spouses may hurl this phrase when one or the other feels wronged. Children wear parents out with this indictment, too, when suggesting a perceived parental favoritism toward another child. Because people are expected to be reasonable and fair with one another, it is not out of line to wonder, is God fair in His dealings with people?

answer

There is a slight but important difference between the Bible's definition of "fair" and "just." God is always just, the Bible says, but God may not always be fair. Hidden within the meaning of *fair* in the English language is the concept of compromise or favor. A bargaining agreement between union and management would be considered fair when both sides give a little bit and compromise. Since God does not compromise and make concessions in His rulings, He might not be considered fair.

However, the word *just* carries with it the underlying concept of truth. A just decision is marked by truth and reason. A just analysis is correct and without error. To say

God is just implies that God is truthful, correct, unbiased, proper, and righteous—all the things the Bible says God is. In fact, Moses sang God's praise, reminding the ancient Israelites that all of God's ways are just. The Babylonian king Nebuchadnezzar praised and exalted God because "everything he does is right and all his ways are just" (Daniel 4:37, NIV). Even the apostle Paul assured the suffering Thessalonians that God was aware of their persecution and trouble. He declared, "God is just: He will pay back trouble to those who trouble you" (2 Thessalonians 1:6, NIV).

Scripture says God may not be fair in His dealings with people. But when God deals with people, He will always be loving, He will always be faithful, and He will always be just.

worth thinking about

▶ **God is just**; He defends the needy, the repentant, and those who have no human supporters.

▶ **Since God is just**, He wants His people to be more than fair in their dealings, too. He wants His children to deal justly with others.

▶ **Though God is just**, His justice may not always be immediately apparent. It may appear that the wicked prosper and the faithless have it easy, but God's justice is coming.

> *Compromise must always be impossible where the truth is essential and fundamental.*
> Charles H. Spurgeon

51

question

▼

Why does God let ungodly people succeed?

In a job interview, a young man was asked to define
success. Predictably he replied, "A good job, a stable
family, and a livable income." Then he added, "To be
truly successful, all of my bosses, including God, would
have to be pleased with my work." Unfortunately, the
position he had applied for was offered to an unprinci-
pled man who happened to have more seniority in the
company. Disappointed, the younger man questioned,
"Why does God let ungodly people succeed?"

answer

▼

The answer to the young man's question is found in the
Bible's definition of *success*, because God and people
have different yardsticks when it comes to measuring
success. People see wealth, position, power, and personal
fulfillment as the hallmarks of success. But God views
these things differently. These signs of success are often
achieved through self-will or self-determination. The
Book of Micah indicates success that comes through self-
determination is built on pride. Paul's letter to the
Ephesians says self-oriented success brings on boasting,
and the Book of Romans adds that such success leads to
ungratefulness and forgetfulness of God.

That is why God does not look at the outward signs as people do. God measures success by the attitude of the heart. To God, self-willed, prideful boasters are not successful people at all, no matter how much money they make. The Bible says a person's faithfulness to God is the most important success factor.

Though outwardly it may appear ungodly people are successful, the Bible says these bits and pieces of wealth and power are all the success the ungodly will ever know. Their achievements will not follow them when they die. Solomon said no one should be concerned when the ungodly succeed or even be envious of them, for the ungodly have "no future—nothing to look forward to" (Proverbs 24:20, GNT). However, those who love God and pursue His ways are guaranteed God's ultimate definition of *success*—the wonders and blessings of heaven.

worth thinking about

▶ Any successfulness that comes through self-effort does not bring glory to God.

▶ Deuteronomy proclaims God as the One who gives the ability to attain wealth. He is the source of all human skill and talent.

▶ David penned Psalm 37 to remind people God is aware of the ways of ungodly people. One day the ungodly will no longer succeed.

> *I don't remember that the Lord ever spoke of success. He spoke only of faithfulness in love. This is the only success that really counts.*
> Mother Teresa

▼

Why does God let bad things happen to good people?

Everyone knew John and liked him. He was willing to help anyone in need anytime. But John seemed to have constant problems. He slipped and broke a hip. Barely recovered from that, his chain saw kicked back and took a chunk out of his leg. Three weeks after the cast was removed, doctors found lung cancer. Where was God in all this? Why did He let these bad things happen to such a nice person?

answer

▼

Some folks think if you make a commitment to do what God wants, you will never have another day of trouble. He will keep all the bad stuff away from you. While that sounds like it should be true, the Bible says the opposite is likely to happen. Why? Because the world is in sin's stranglehold.

God gave the first man and woman a perfect home—no problems, no sickness, no bad weather. But by choice these first two people introduced the world to wrongdoing and its effects of disease and death. The Bible says from that time until this, all people have suffered. That is the way life is in a sinful world, and therein lies the answer to why bad things happen to good people. In a sinful world, darkness seeks to put out the light. In a sinful world, bad behavior is left unpunished. In a sinful world, good people are laughed at. In a sinful world, God is insulted and mocked.

But in a sinful world, God offers hope. The Bible assures you your suffering can become profitable when God is your life center. The Book of James indicates suffering is a character builder. It has the ability to deepen fellowship among believers. The apostles Peter and Paul indicated in their letters that suffering can also help you develop a deeper trust in God. Through suffering you are drawn closer to Him, and thus are more completely prepared for eternal life in heaven.

worth thinking about

▶ **Suffering can help** equip God's children for more effective service to one another and to those who do not know God.

▶ **Suffering is an indicator** of the price that must be paid for godliness, for sometimes suffering can be God's chastisement to help a person grow in faith.

▶ **God understands** the emotional burden of suffering and promises comfort and rest to His suffering children. That comfort is accessible through prayer.

> *Your pain has a purpose . . . something you will discover in your own walk with God. It may be a marvelous discovery, a grace, like Paul's, which once received makes you glad you went down the road of suffering with God at your side.*
>
> John Haggai

question

▼

Does God want people to be afraid of Him?

An elderly person may be hesitant to walk on icy streets during the winter, fearing a slip, fall, and broken bones. A person may be afraid to climb aboard an airliner that has not passed its safety certification. A child may be fearful of walking past a dog that barks and bares its fangs. Folks need to be afraid of some things. Yet where does God fit into the fear equation? Does God want people to be afraid of Him?

answer

▼

Fear is a natural reaction to a person, place, or thing that threatens an individual. The Bible indicates such fear is appropriate when one is confronted with God. Jesus told His disciples they should fear God more than they feared people because God has the power to send someone to hell. God is not someone to be taken lightly, since He holds ultimate power over your life. In that sense, then, God does want people to be afraid of Him.

Yet the Bible says your fear of God can be the means to a deeper trust in Him. When that happens, terror is transformed into reverence, awe, and respect for God. Genesis says that happened to Jacob. As Jacob prepared for bed, a strong adversary attacked him and wrestled him to the ground. All night long, the two fought until Jacob's adversary said, "Enough!" By then Jacob had realized he was wrestling with God. Any time during the wrestling match God could have snuffed out Jacob's life, but He did not. And Jacob, recognizing that fact, held more tightly to God, refusing to let Him go until God blessed him. What began in Jacob as a deep-seated fear for his life was replaced with a deeper trust in God and a longing for His goodness. Being fearful of what God can do to you can become the means for bringing you closer to Him, too. The Bible promises God will always bless those who fear and reverence Him.

worth thinking about

▶ **The Bible says** the fear of God is to be seen and expressed by God's children in their words, actions, and worship.

▶ **The fear of God** will act as a key to unlock the treasures of salvation, wisdom, and knowledge and to help build a sure foundation for your life.

▶ **The Bible says** possessing a fear of God will lead to a proper respect for others, a positive attitude toward work, and a building of right relationships among God's people.

> *Some people think that God peers over the balcony of heaven trying to find anybody who is enjoying life. And when He spots a happy person, He yells, "Now cut that out!" That concept of God should make us shudder because it is blasphemous.*
>
> Paul Little

54 question

Will God bring world peace in this century?

It was called "the war to end all wars." Unfortunately, World War II was not the last war between the nations of the world. Armed conflicts in Korea, Vietnam, Bosnia, the Middle East, and elsewhere keep the images of war on television news programs and the front pages of newspapers. Yet peaceful coexistence between nations is the aim of many people. Since God also desires peace, will He help these efforts and bring about world peace in this century?

answer

The Bible promises a time of world peace. However, the Book of Daniel says the world will be very unpeaceful before peace comes. There will be wars and disputes among nations. The New Testament says people will be self-absorbed, money-hungry, crude, coarse, self-promoting, cynical, and ruthless. They will pretend to be religious, yet disobey their parents. Many will be smooth talkers who persuade the unstable and needy and take advantage of them. Yet the Bible says God will change all this. He will bring peace to the world. When? Will it happen in this century?

No one knows the exact time except God Himself, but the Book of Romans says that time gets closer every day. When God finally says, "Time's up!" everything unpeaceful will end. Then God will set up a kingdom on earth that will be different from any other form of government. God's kingdom will be a kingdom of peace, ensuring harmony between all nations of the world. The Book of Revelation says this peaceful time on earth will last for a thousand years.

Until that time, however, worldwide peace will continue to elude treaty makers. So God asks His children to help ready the world for His peaceable kingdom: Pray for the peace of Jerusalem. Love one another. Live in unity. These attempts for peace will focus hearts on God. Only He can bring worldwide peace. And one day He will.

worth thinking about

▶ **Some Bible scholars** suggest that Jesus' teaching in Matthew 5–7 gives insight into what life will be like in God's peaceable kingdom on earth.

▶ **The prophet Isaiah** says when God brings peace to the world, those thousand years will also be a time of great prosperity.

▶ **Humanity's search** for peace can change with circumstance. Jeremiah said the desire for peace increases during times of difficulty, whereas times of ease make people less interested in seeking peace.

> *The only way God could impose peace on the world would be to robotize our wills and rob every human being of the power of choice. He has not chosen to do that. He has given every person a free will.*
>
> John Haggai

55

What does God do to people who break His laws?

If a driver operates a motor vehicle while under the influence of drugs or alcohol and is flagged down by a police officer, a ticket and court appearance will be forthcoming. If a teenager does not come home by curfew, it might cost that teen extra chores or a removal of privileges. Why? There is a penalty to pay for breaking the law—whether on the highway or at home. But what does God do to people who break His laws?

answer

The Book of Joshua goes into detail about the blessings God promises to send His people if they follow His ways. But just after the list of blessings come some sobering words. If God's people break His laws or refuse to follow His ways, God promises there will be punishment.

Leviticus 26 categorized these punishments into penalty clusters or groupings. For example, if God's people broke His laws just a little bit or for a short time, they would be punished with only sudden terrors, wasting diseases, burning fevers, failing eyesight, and prevailing enemies who would devour every crop in the fields. If God's people continued to sin, however, the punishments would escalate. There would be no rain and virtually no crops.

Wild animals would roam unchecked, killing small children and cattle. People would be fearful to travel. If God's people still would not turn back to Him and follow His laws, the severity of God's punishments would increase again. God would send other nations to terrorize His people. Cities would become places of plague and ruin. Food supplies would be rationed. People would starve to death. The land would be devastated and desolate.

Deuteronomy echoes these serious words, reminding God's people, "If you refuse to listen to the LORD your God and do not obey all the commands and decrees I am giving you today, all these curses will come and overwhelm you" (Deuteronomy 28:15, NLT). Scripture is clear: God will punish those who break His laws.

worth thinking about

▶ **Paul reminded readers** that God is just. If God judges others for doing wrong, He will also judge you if you do wrong.

▶ **One day God** will judge all people according to what they have done. He will bless those who do good, but punish those who refuse to obey Him.

▶ **The Bible says** refusing to follow God's ways is wrong. It is an act of disobedience. But Romans and Ephesians say disobedience, like all sin, can be forgiven.

> *As long as we work on God's line, He will aid us. When we attempt to work on our own lines, He rebukes us with failure.*
>
> Theodore Ledyard Cuyler

Is God fair in His dealings with people?

An extravaganza before God
as he comes, as he comes
to set everything right on earth,
set everything right, treat
everyone fair.

Psalm 96:13, THE MESSAGE

56 question
What does God want people to do when they do wrong?

Run the gas tank to empty on your vehicle, and it will not start. Blow a transformer on a power pole, and a neighborhood will lose electricity. To remedy these negative circumstances requires a proactive strategy. The vehicle will need fuel; the transformer will need replacing. According to the Bible, people also need a proactive strategy when they do bad things or refuse to follow God's way. So what does God want people to do when they do wrong?

answer

The Bible prescribes two steps to follow if you have done something wrong or have not followed the ways and will of God. The first step is to turn away from any wrongdoing. For example, Ezra encouraged the ancient Israelites to abandon the false gods they had begun to worship while in captivity in Babylon. The Book of Numbers also indicates you need to prayerfully speak to God about any wrongdoing and make appropriate restitution where necessary.

Though turning away from wrongdoing is an important first step, the Bible says God also expects a full turning of your heart toward Him. Ezekiel said this second step of turning toward God becomes a true work of obedience, of doing what God wants you to do. Jeremiah reminded God's children to go beyond showing remorse over wrong to working out a change in behavior. Daniel echoed this thought, saying a heart that is turned toward God will exhibit itself in a life that is lived by God's principles. Isaiah added that turning away from wrongdoing and turning toward God will result in a deeper faith in Him.

Too often people wish to cleanse their consciences but not change their ways. Both steps are necessary if an individual wants to have full fellowship with God. The Bible says these steps of repentance for wrongdoing are the only ways to escape God's judgment and receive the forgiveness and restoration He offers.

worth thinking about

▶ According to Psalms, a true turning away from sin is often marked by a sense of sorrow for wrongdoing.

▶ True repentance must be sincere. The Bible reminds readers God does not want any wavering between good and bad. God says choose the good and stick to it.

▶ The Bible resounds with the news that the steps of repentance open the way for God's blessings to fall on His children.

> If they pray to me and repent and turn away from the evil they have been doing, then I will hear them in heaven, forgive their sins, and make their land prosperous again.
>
> 2 Chronicles 7:14, GNT

57

question

Does God forgive everyone who sins?

Jesus told the story of a son who left home and spent his inheritance on wasteful living. After making many bad choices, the son ended up far from home, penniless, and starving. Recognizing his life would be better as a laborer on his father's farm, the son went home. When his father saw him coming, he ran to meet the wayward son and welcomed him. Jesus said God is the father in this story, for God stands ready to forgive everyone.

answer

Will God really forgive everyone who sins? The Bible gives a conditional yes to this question. Every person needs forgiveness at some time in life. The Book of Numbers indicates God's nature includes the openhanded willingness to forgive. And the Book of Hebrews declares God promises to grant forgiveness.

However, there is a catch. God will not give forgiveness unless He is asked for it. Think of it this way. A parent is able to give a child a glass of milk, a crayon, or a push on a swing. Yet parents teach children to ask for these things. These things are readily available to the child, but will not be given unless requested. The Bible says forgiveness is applied in the same way. A person has to recognize the need for forgiveness and ask for it before God will perform it. The apostle Peter said God waits for those who are stubborn and willful, for those who turn from what God wants them to do. God waits and is saddened that these do not quickly turn away from sin and ask for His forgiveness.

Indeed, God stands ready to forgive everyone who sins. He will freely, graciously, and quickly forgive the moment anyone seeks His forgiveness. The Book of 1 John says all you have to do is acknowledge your wrongdoing and ask God to forgive. He will be faithful and do it.

worth thinking about

▶ **Those who refuse** to turn from wrongdoing and continue to make bad choices make God unhappy. He longs to grant the freedom, joy, and completeness of heart that come with His forgiveness.

▶ **For those who** sincerely turn from wrongdoing, God gives a wonderful promise. The Bible says when God forgives wrongdoing, He promises to forget it, too. (See Hebrews 8:12.)

▶ **The Bible says** God's forgiveness turns sin and evil in a person's life into an opportunity for a greater understanding of God's goodness and grace.

> *When our hearts are contrite, humble, and open—when we sincerely repent all our wrongdoing—God forgives. And when He forgives, He does so not meagerly and reluctantly, but gracefully and abundantly.*
>
> F. B. Meyer

58 question

Why would God let people go to hell?

Amusement parks often post signs at the entrances of certain rides advising people of the dangers of the ride. Pregnant women, small children, people with heart conditions, etc., are advised to avoid the ride. Park owners do not want these people on these rides because of possible serious side effects. The Bible says an eternity spent in hell is the serious side effect of living a wicked lifestyle. So why would God let people go to hell?

answer

If you have ever watched someone ignore the warnings at an amusement park ride and then exit the ride with severe pain or illness, you have seen why some people will go to hell. It is a sad and unpleasant fact. Some folks will make choices that will put them in harm's way regardless of posted warning signs. The Bible says the same principle applies to choices made about spiritual things. The Bible contains warnings about the dangers of following certain lifestyles. The Book of Galatians states that good choices based on God's recommendations will bring about a wonderful eternity. However, poor choices based on selfish, wicked ideas will usher in an eternity of suffering. The Gospels add that God never forces anyone to go to hell. If people end up there, they do so by their own choice.

Since God cannot coexist with anything evil, Revelation says He prepared hell as a place for the devil and his demons to spend eternity. Hell was never intended to be anyone else's eternal home, but the Bible indicates an eternity spent in hell is the consequence any person can expect if God and His ways are rejected.

Just as posted placards in the amusement park warn people away from dangerous rides, so the Bible raises warning signs to guide people away from wrongdoing. To avoid the serious side effect of hell, one must pay attention to the Bible's warning signs and follow God's ways instead.

worth thinking about

▶ **Though hell** will be a final, eternal home for many, people can turn away from hell at any time before death and find an assurance of heaven.

▶ **The Bible portrays** God as a gentleman, never brutally imposing His will upon anyone but rather giving people the opportunity to choose their ultimate destiny.

▶ **God has left** guideposts and warning signs throughout creation to help people choose to do right and avoid an eternity in hell.

> *As the enjoyment of God is the heaven of the Saints, so the loss of God is the hell of the ungodly. And, as the enjoying of God is the enjoying of all, so the loss of God is the loss of all.*
> Richard Baxter

question

Does God care how you treat other people?

Referees at sporting events enforce penalties for certain misbehaviors. A hockey player may spend time in the penalty box for high-sticking. A basketball player may be awarded a free shot if fouled by an opposing team member. An entire football team may find itself sent back several yards if a referee calls a holding penalty. Behavior matters in sporting events, but what about in life? Does your behavior matter to God? Does He care how you treat other people?

answer

God does care how people treat each other. In the law God gave Moses on Mount Sinai, six of the ten commands deal with interpersonal relationships. According to Exodus 20, God's people are to respect and honor their parents and remain faithful to their marriage vows. They are forbidden to accuse anyone falsely or to steal from one another. They are to refrain from committing murder or desiring anything that anyone else possesses. God instituted these Ten Commandments with the provision that His children would be blessed if they followed these laws and treated other people as God wanted them to be treated.

But God does not stop there. He speaks throughout the Bible, urging His people in the Psalms to live together in unity. He begs His children in Zechariah to be united in worship, and entreats them in Jeremiah to actively work for reconciliation between estranged families and nations.

The Book of James speaks directly to the behavior of those who discriminate based on outward appearance, reminding readers to treat everyone the same. Peter encouraged God's people to show hospitality and love to all. Matthew said God's children should care for the sick and those in prison. And Paul encouraged forgiveness for a runaway slave when society said judgment was in order.

Above all, God wants His children to show others His "love, joy, peace, patience, kindness, goodness, faithfulness, humility, and self-control. There is no law against such things as these" (Galatians 5:22–23, GNT).

worth thinking about

▶ **The Bible reminds** God's people to be faithfully committed to one another, regardless of personal situation or the convenience of doing so.

▶ **God wants His** people to be united in mind and purpose so that others who do not know God will want that peace and harmony, too.

▶ **Because God** has taken the initiative to love everyone, He expects His people to follow His example and love others, too.

> *Talk and act like a person expecting to be judged by the Rule that sets us free. For if you refuse to act kindly, you can hardly expect to be treated kindly.*
>
> James 2:12–13, THE MESSAGE

question

Does God ever get tired of judging all the time?

Assembly line workers take regularly scheduled breaks to alleviate the monotony and tiresomeness of their work. Doing the same thing the same way repeatedly for a long period is wearing. It is true of any job. But is this true for God, too? He spends all day every day watching over everyone in the world to see whether folks are good or bad. So does God get tired of judging people all the time?

answer

The psalmist declared God never sleeps or even takes a nap. Isaiah insisted God never gets tired or worn out, either. So, in answering the first half of this question, the Bible is adamant: God never gets tired of doing anything He chooses to do.

The second half of this question suggests all of God's time is spent judging people. In reality, God does not judge people all the time. According to the Bible, God has other work to do, too. The psalmist said God's work includes providing the world's needs as well as giving special care to His children. The Old Testament prophets stated God's work also includes saving and delivering His people from sin, death, problems, and difficulties. The Book of Job celebrates God as the Creator and sustainer of the universe. While the world was begun long ago, God is still at work in creation every day. The Bible says God is the One who holds all of creation together.

Yet God's work also includes the carrying out of discipline, punishment, and judgment. God has the authority to administer these forms of correction because the world is His kingdom. Therefore, the prophet Ezekiel says God evaluates and disciplines every individual. The Book of Joshua indicates God punishes whole families. The prophet Joel declares God reproves the nations. And the Book of Revelation says at the end of time God will eventually judge all people based on the way they have lived their lives.

worth thinking about

▶ **Part of God's** ongoing work in this world is His timely punishment of ungodly individuals such as Belshazzar in the Book of Daniel and King Jehoram in 2 Chronicles.

▶ **The Bible says** God's judgment at the end of time will serve several purposes: to display God's glory, vindicate the righteous, defend the weak, and punish wrongdoing.

▶ **Interaction between people** causes ripple effects like tossing a pebble into a puddle. Only when time ends will everyone see how others have been influenced by their attitudes and actions. Then God will judge the world.

> *God will judge men justly, and they will not be able to raise their voices because of the base upon which He judges them.*
> Francis Schaeffer

61

question

Did God really create everything?

The third-grade science project was titled "Rocket Propulsion to Mars." The exhibit held charts, rocket pieces, timelines, and glossy photographs illustrating how an astronaut could get to Mars. It was an impressive project, so the teacher asked the student, "Did you do this yourself?" The student replied, "Yes, I did! Daddy only helped a little." The creation of the universe and everything in it is an impressive project, too. But did God really create everything by Himself?

answer

The Bible says yes. Great paintings and elementary school science projects usually have the name of the artist or project manager affixed to the work in some way to give clear indication of who created the piece. However, the elements of the universe, including the planets, stars, and all the inhabitants on this planet, bear no clear signature of their creator. So how can you know God created everything?

The Bible says so. The Book of Genesis declares God as the only Creator of everything in the world, giving God glory for creating light and darkness. The prophet Amos says God alone was the originator of everything in the heavens. The Psalms extol God's greatness in forming the land, the sea, and the creatures that inhabit both domains. And Hebrews expands this information by adding that no one but God created everything in the universe, too.

Indeed, the Bible proclaims God created everything. And God has given proofs of His work in creation, too. Though God may not have placed His name on every work of creation, Genesis says God has placed something like a signature on humanity, stamping His image on every human being. The Book of Romans says the created order of things in plants and animals is a visible witness to God's systematic nature and kindly character. And the Book of Daniel declares the continuation of this natural world is yet another proof of God's singular, creative power.

worth thinking about

▶ The Genesis creation story witnesses to God's sense of order as each thing in creation progresses from the least complex (light and darkness) to the most complex (a human being).

▶ A satellite sent into space in the 1990s confirmed the big bang beginning of the universe, but Genesis says it was God who set off the explosion.

▶ The Bible proclaims the world was created out of nothing by the will of God, the word of God, the hand of God, and the mind of God.

> *What can be more foolish than to think that all this rare fabric of heaven and earth could come by chance, when all the skill of science is not able to make an oyster.*
> Jeremy Taylor

question

Is God detached from the world He created?

In a laboratory a scientist might set up a bacterial experiment in a petri dish on a Monday and not look at that experiment again until a week later. The scientist knows that it takes time to grow bacteria to a point that they can be studied, so during that passage of time the scientist would pay attention to other things. Is God like this scientist? Is He detached from the world He created and paying attention to other things?

answer

The answer to this question is clear-cut. Many passages in the Bible state God is actively involved in everything He has made.

Centuries before Jesus Christ was born, God's activity and involvement in the world were revealed through creation and the nation of Israel. The Book of Genesis illustrates God's activity in making the universe. The Psalms show God's involvement in sustaining everything He made by keeping everything in working order. The Book of Job presents multiple passages that demonstrate God's activity in changing the weather, controlling the oceans, and ordering the movement of the stars. Exodus reminds readers that God was the One who actively called out the

When Jesus lived on the earth, God's activity was revealed in the response of people to Jesus' message and in the miracles that accompanied Jesus' trial, crucifixion, and death. From the time of Jesus until the present, God's activity has been revealed in the life of the church and the lives of God's children. The Book of Acts declares God is the One who determines the course of the nations. He is active in the lives of individuals, too. And Paul reminded readers in Corinth that God's children can sense God's Spirit working through their lives when they use the special talents God has given each one.

worth thinking about

▶ **If you study** the names of God, you will see that His names reflect His nature and His involvement in His children's lives.

▶ **God is active** by nature and actively works out His plans and purposes in all of creation.

▶ **The Bible**—God's written word—is active, too. It is not just a communication of theoretical truth; it is an active, powerful force in the world that can change lives forever.

> *God has not created his universe just to watch it wind down without any attention given to it. He continues to be involved.*
> Gabrielle Eden

question

Can God do whatever He wants whenever He wants to do it?

Parents tell children what to do. Professors tell students what to do. Bosses at work tell employees what to do. Chief executive officers tell bosses what to do. It seems there is always somebody higher up who can tell someone at a lower level what to do. But what about God? Since He is God and does not have a parent, boss, or chief executive officer, can He do whatever He wants whenever He wants to do it?

answer

According to the Bible, yes, He can! God is able to do whatever He wants whenever He wants to do it because He rules over all creation. Daniel said God "does as he pleases among the angels of heaven and among the people of the earth. No one can stop him or say to him, 'What do you mean by doing these things?'" (Daniel 4:35, NLT). The Bible says God is like a master Potter and people are His clay creations. A clay milk jug does not tell its potter to make its handle bigger or paint it a different color. The potter is the one who chooses to make a rounded handle or a squared-off lip. In the same manner, God has every right to exercise His judgment on what will happen to people.

The Bible also says that since God can do whatever He wants, He cannot be successfully opposed. His sovereignty extends over all things, all history, and all forces of evil. In the Old Testament, Hannah recognized this and declared, "Those who fight against the LORD will be shattered" (1 Samuel 2:10, NLT). A Jewish teacher in Jesus' day urged Jewish council members to leave Jesus' followers alone. He said it would be fruitless to try to fight against something God had set in motion. Job also recognized God's sovereignty as he proclaimed, "I know that you can do all things; no plan of yours can be thwarted" (Job 42:2, NIV).

worth thinking about

▶ Although God can do whatever He wants, Revelation says He stands at the door of your heart and knocks. He will not force His way into your life. He waits for you to invite Him in.

▶ Since God can do whatever He wants, He could let wars devastate the earth. But Mark says God chooses to exercise compassion and spare people from total destruction.

▶ In reality, there is only one thing God cannot do—He cannot be unfaithful to His character. Therefore, God will always be loving, kind, just, holy, true, faithful, and good.

> I know that our LORD is great, greater than
> all the gods. He does whatever he wishes
> in heaven and on earth, in the seas
> and in the depths below.
> Psalm 135:5–6, GNT

question

Does God micromanage your life?

A popular comic strip depicts a common office worker whose every movement comes under the scrutiny of an overbearing supervisor. The comic is so popular because many people work for bosses who feel the need to micromanage every aspect of a job to ensure it is completed correctly and in the exact way the boss proscribes. Since the Bible says God is in control of everything, does that mean God micromanages all the details of your life, too?

answer

You are no Dilbert, and God is no micromanager. Micromanaging involves directing or controlling something in a meddlesome manner with excessive attention given to minor details. Although God is in control of everything in the world, He does not micromanage, nor does He treat people as if they were rats in a maze, all running for the same piece of cheese. He would never use people like puppets on strings or robots that moved at His every whim and command. Yes, God *is* in control of everything. Many passages in both the Old and New Testaments of the Bible agree to that. But the Bible also indicates God gives people choices.

People matter to God, so God treats people with love. In fact, the Book of Jeremiah says God has a loving plan for everyone on earth. He wants people to join Him in heaven one day, so God has laid out a heavenly path for people to follow. Jesus' stories in the Gospels illustrate people's options either to follow God's way or to reject it. Yet Isaiah reminds readers that God willingly gives guidance to help people stay on His heavenly path.

God does not micromanage every detail of life. But Jesus reminded people it is to their advantage to let God have His way in their lives. Jesus said this was the only way to ensure they would be walking the narrow pathway to heaven and not the wide expressway to hell.

worth thinking about

▶ **The Bible assures** readers God will give each individual what he or she needs most and will coordinate events to bring about these positive blessings.

▶ **Even if God's intentions** are not clear when you are going through a tough time, He is deeply concerned about the choices you make and the details of your life.

▶ **The Bible says** God's plan for your life will be carried out through His control of circumstances and situations.

> *I will instruct you and show you the way to go;*
> *with My eye on you, I will give counsel.*
> Psalm 32:8, HCSB

question

▼

Is God too busy ruling the world to bother with one person?

In Charles Dickens's story *A Christmas Carol*, one of the major players, Mrs. Cratchit, was very busy on Christmas morning, trying to cook a special dinner for her family. As you read the story, it becomes clear that Mrs. Cratchit was so busy with Martha's arrival she missed Peter's mess-making as he stirred the potatoes. Does this ever happen to God? Is He too busy ruling the world to notice or bother with one person?

answer

▼

The Bible says God does watch over the details of the world. He sets up nations. He holds back the tides from swallowing the earth. He sends rain, wind, and clouds. But the Bible also says God is involved with His children—every single one of them. God is in the individual business. Genesis says He created the first human being in His own likeness. Exodus says God and Moses were friends who spoke together. Leviticus says God called Aaron and set him apart to be God's first high priest. Hebrews adds that God took note of Abraham, too, declaring him righteous and granting him blessings.

But there is more. Matthew lists the genealogy of Jesus, naming all the individuals who were the human forebears of Jesus' mother, Mary. David says in the Psalms that God watched over David's life, keeping him safe, blessing his household, and granting him peace. God remembered Ruth for her commitment to family. Deborah is commended for her leadership over Israel. Sarah, Hannah, and Elizabeth received God's favor and the ability to bear children.

And the Bible declares God's intent to occasion good things in your life, too. The Book of Romans says God has given you special gifts based on the plan He has for your life. Matthew says God cares so much about you, He knows how many hairs are on your head. Truly, individuals are important to God.

worth thinking about

▶ **God is concerned** about the daily details of His children's lives. The psalmist said God is familiar with those who are His and knows what they think and say and do.

▶ **God cares** for individuals. He remembered each Jew who returned from captivity and inspired Ezra to write down the name of each one.

▶ **God's personalized** attention begins here on earth but continues in heaven. Revelation says when God's children get to heaven, each child will receive a new name that God has chosen for each one.

> *I have had so many evidences of His direction, so many instances when I have been controlled by some other power than my own will, that I cannot doubt that this power comes from above.*
>
> Abraham Lincoln

Is anything too hard for God to do?

Dear GOD, my Master, you created earth and sky by your great power—by merely stretching out your arm! There is nothing you can't do.

Jeremiah 32:17, THE MESSAGE

question

What does God tell people to rule over?

When a boss leaves the office for an extended period—a vacation, a business trip, a medical leave, etc.—projects or tasks may be given out to other people in the office. While the boss is away these folks act in the boss's place, making decisions, following up the details, and making sure the work gets done. Since God is not physically present on this planet, He has directed people to rule over some things for Him, too.

answer

The first chapter of Genesis indicates humanity's first delegated position: Adam was given the responsibility of naming all the living creatures of the earth and then was commissioned to rule over them. That was a tall order, but God did not stop there. Proverbs says God urges wise parents to rule fairly over their children. And knowing that people can be insensitive and ruthless toward each other, Leviticus says God told people to rule those who work for them with the same kindness God shows to His children.

God has also given humanity the responsibility of ruling one another. The Book of Daniel says God is the originator of civil authorities who, acting as God's representatives, govern groups of people and rule over them. Proverbs says

God gives these rulers the authority to originate laws for people to follow, too. And the Book of Romans reminds those who have been given such authority by God that they are God's servants, appointed by God to act as earthly representatives of God's heavenly court.

Several Bible passages also say that God's children will be given positions of ruling authority at the end of time. The psalmist said the godly will one day rule over the ungodly. Isaiah says those in captivity will one day rule over their captors. And 2 Timothy declares that those children of God who are faithful despite trouble and persecution will rule the world with Jesus Christ for a thousand years when He returns to earth.

worth thinking about

- ▶ **God gave people** dominion of the inferior creatures of the world, over fish, and over all the birds. Though God provides the needs of these creatures, God has directed people to take care of them.

- ▶ **God wants people** to be careful of the words they say. Too many times folks praise God one moment and curse others the next. The tongue needs to be ruled.

- ▶ **God wants people** to rule themselves, too. Knowing God and following His ways should lead to self-control.

Be responsible for fish in the sea and birds in the air, for every living thing that moves on the face of Earth.
Genesis 1:28, THE MESSAGE

67

question

Will God ever give up?

You have probably said, "I give up" in response to a riddle, a chess game, or an overzealous tickling match or pillow fight. It seems people are prone to giving up. Some folks give up when a job is too difficult to complete. Others give up when they repeatedly fail at a specific task. Still others give up when they recognize the course they are following could be dangerous. But will God ever give up?

answer

The Bible says God will never give up because He cannot. The Book of Numbers says God is not a man, nor does He behave like one. Psalms contends God's unchangeable, eternal character makes it impossible for God to give up. And Hebrews declares that even if everyone in the world died and the mountains wasted away, God would still be the faithful, unchanging God who never stops loving, never stops forgiving.

Indeed, the Bible says God's nature is incapable of quitting, incapable of giving up on His children. The prophet Isaiah says nothing can stop God from sharing His love and righteousness with thousands of generations of those who love Him. God will never give up providing eternal life for His people because He "is more powerful than anyone else" (John 10:29, NLT). Lamentations says God's mercies never fail, Psalms states His faithfulness continues through the generations, and Titus resounds with the hope of eternal life that God will never give up giving.

God is changeless, James says. He is the One "who is, and who was, and who is to come" (Revelation 1:8, NIV). Jeremiah says God will never stop doing good to His children. Matthew adds that He will never betray His faithfulness, violate His covenant, or alter what He has spoken. And 2 Thessalonians declares God will never quit strengthening His children and protecting them from the evil one. Our God is a God who never quits.

worth thinking about

▶ God never gave up keeping His promise to Abraham. Even when Abraham and Sarah were past their childbearing years, Abraham believed God and was given the child God promised.

▶ Too often people persist in following a course of action or belief that is contrary to God's will and ways. The Bible says God is even more persistent in urging such people to repent.

▶ The Bible says God is Love. He will never give up "keeping his covenant of love to a thousand generations of those who love him and keep his commands" (Deuteronomy 7:9, NIV).

> *God, who got you started in this spiritual adventure, shares with us the life of his Son and our Master Jesus. He will never give up on you. Never forget that.*
>
> 1 Corinthians 1:9, THE MESSAGE

68 question

Why does God allow miracles?

The dictionary defines a miracle as an event that is out of the ordinary, one that cannot be explained by natural occurrences. For example, if a doctor tells a patient there is no hope for healing but the patient makes a full recovery, doctor and patient would agree that a miracle occurred. Such instances are rare, but many people know folks who profess to have experienced a miracle of some kind. So why does God allow miracles?

answer

The Bible says miracles happen for many reasons. The Psalms indicate miracles are demonstrations of the presence and power of God in the world. The Book of Numbers adds that miracles sometimes serve as God's vehicles for the judgment of people and nations. Several passages in the New Testament state that miracles are also a part of God's plan of redemption. For example, God verified Jesus' message of the gospel and the promise of salvation "by signs, wonders and various miracles" (Hebrews 2:4, NIV).

God also allows miracles for the benefit of His children. Exodus recounts God's miraculous provision of food, water, and protection for the ancient Israelites as they traveled in the wilderness of Sinai. The accounts in Joshua mention God's miracles that brought about military victories for His people. Miraculous births are recorded throughout the pages of the Bible, and miracles of healing are scattered throughout the Old and New Testaments.

Miracles in the Bible also occur as markers of special times or situations. The Book of Exodus records several significant miracles during the time of the Israelites' departure from Egypt. The narratives of the Kings and Chronicles recount God's miraculous intervention during times of military siege and religious crisis. And the Gospels journal the life of Jesus and the miracles that accompanied His time on earth. Indeed, all of God's miracles confirm His presence, power, and authority over all things. God is a miracle worker.

worth thinking about

▶ **The Bible says** miracles are not always a proof of God's work. The devil can counterfeit many of God's miracles.

▶ **The Gospels say** miracles are not always a proof of genuine faith. A person may perform miracles but not be a true child of God.

▶ **In addition,** God's miracles are gifts given by His sovereign will to authenticate the message of His spokespeople.

> *Because of their unbelief, he couldn't do any mighty miracles among them except to place his hands on a few sick people and heal them.*
>
> Mark 6:5, NLT

69

question
▼

Why does God keep His children here on earth?

When two people get married, they usually leave the wedding festivities and head off on a honeymoon. When a person takes a new job, a change of office or work location is usually in order. When students progress from high school to college, they leave one campus and begin their studies on another. However, when people become God's children, they do not leave earth and move on immediately to heaven. Why not? Why does God keep His kids here on earth?

answer
▼

All people play a part in God's plan for this world. Every person has had a job to do from the time of the first man, Adam. Genesis says God "placed the man in the Garden of Eden to cultivate it and guard it" (Genesis 2:15, GNT). Although God wanted Adam to enjoy a personal relationship with Him, Adam's existence had a purpose beyond companionship. Adam was to be God's gardener in Eden. And Adam continued working the land outside the Garden of Eden until he died.

Jesus' life reflects this concept, too. In the Gospel of John, Jesus told His disciples that He found nourishment in doing God's will and in finishing God's work. When is finished," only then did He depart this life because He had completed the work of redemption. His death was a vital part of the work God had given Him to do.

The same essential principle applies today. It does not matter whether you are healthy, wealthy, in a good social position, or not. God's children remain on earth to fulfill the job God has given each one to do. What is that job? To be Christ's ambassadors—a position each child will hold until God calls each one to heaven.

worth thinking about

▶ **What kind** of a world would it be if God took His children immediately to heaven? Without anyone to exhibit God's righteousness, the world would be bound by hopelessness and fear.

▶ **According to Ephesians,** God leaves His children on earth to bring glory and honor to Him by the way they live.

▶ **The apostle Peter** reminded readers that God's children are here on earth to "show others the goodness of God" (1 Peter 2:9, NLT).

> *God has a purpose for the rest of our time on Planet Earth—and it isn't to make money. God leaves us here because He wants others to come to know His love and mercy through our witness.*
> Eddie Rasnake

question

How has God shown Himself to be all-powerful?

In a strongman competition, one contestant bent to lift barbells that were heavier than twice his body weight. Across the stadium, another competitor attempted to pull a school bus as far as he could. Still another participant attempted the brute-strength bending of a steel beam. Throughout the venue people cheered. Feats of strength have always impressed audiences. In the arena of this world, how has God shown Himself to be all-powerful?

answer

God's strength and power go beyond anything a human being could ever accomplish. According to the Bible, God can wipe out nations with one hand, so measuring the limits of God's power is beyond a person's ability. Yet God has proven the scope of His power in many ways.

The prophet Isaiah said God is so powerful, if He has planned it, it will happen; if He has purposed it, it will stand. The Psalms say God is so powerful He does whatever pleases Him in heaven and on earth. And the Book of Daniel adds God is so powerful "no one can hold back his hand or say to him: 'What have you done?'" (Daniel 4:35, NIV).

God's power is also seen in the narratives of the Bible. In Judges, God told Gideon to pare back his army to three hundred men to fight an enemy that could not be numbered. God insisted on the small army to prove His powerful ability to deliver Gideon and the Israelites. In Exodus, the Israelites were trapped between the Red Sea and a large army of Egyptians. God powerfully parted the water so His people could escape. When the army charged in after them, God let the water fall back on top of them, stopping their advance. In the Book of Acts, God powerfully poured His Spirit on Jesus' followers so they could boldly tell people of God's goodness. The pages of the Bible resound with the message: all-surpassing power belongs to God.

worth thinking about

▶ When Israel was enslaved in Egypt, God told Pharaoh He had placed him in power over Egypt so God could demonstrate His power and bring glory to His name.

▶ God's great power is seen in creation—in its variety, its detail, and its continuance. Only a powerful creator could turn dirt into a human being.

▶ God's great power is seen in Christ's resurrection. By bringing Jesus back to life, God demonstrated His supreme power over death and hell.

This, if duly considered, would keep the world in awe of the Lord and His goodness: that the waters of the sea would soon cover the earth if God did not restrain them.

Matthew Henry

71

Is anything too hard for God to do?

If a jar top is sealed too tightly at the factory, it can be too hard for someone to open, especially if the person has arthritis of the hand or fingers. If someone has a limited understanding of a foreign language, it might be too hard for that person to comprehend what a newscaster might say in that language. People sometimes experience things that are too hard to do. But is there anything too hard for God to do?

answer

The Bible is clear about the extent of God's mighty power. Zephaniah states that only God has the power to save and deliver, while the psalmist said only God has the power to be everywhere at once. The Book of Matthew reveals that God's power is stronger than the devil's power, too. When Moses performed God's miracles to convince the ruler of Egypt to free the Israelites, the devil granted power to this pharaoh's magicians to perform the same miracles—with a few notable exceptions. Exodus says the evil magicians could not bring a plague of gnats nor could they kill only the firstborn of every family. God could do both, however, because only He is powerful enough to create, sustain, and take life.

plish something. God is strong enough to do anything He wishes. However, God's power is limited by His character. God cannot do anything that would go against His nature. It is not that it is too hard for Him to do these things—it is impossible for Him to do them! So what are God's impossibilities?

The Book of James says God cannot deny Himself or be tempted in any way. Paul's letter to the Galatians adds that God cannot be mocked. The prophet Habakkuk declared that God cannot tolerate evil, and 1 Samuel states that God cannot lie. Thankfully, all-powerful God cannot be unfaithful to Himself.

worth thinking about

▶ **God is unable** to change His nature. What He has been, He is now and always will be.

▶ **God is unable** to leave His people. He has always been with them and always will be.

▶ **It is not too** hard for God to keep His promises, either. In fact, the Bible says it is impossible for God to go against them. He is powerful enough to keep each one.

> *Ah Lord God, Thou has made the heavens and the earth by Thine outstretched arm. Nothing is too difficult for Thee.*
> Kay Chance

What does God's power accomplish?

A television commercial once featured a bald genie that towered over a clueless woman. The little woman clutched an overflowing laundry basket and looked to the genie for help. In the background, a spokesperson's voice extolled the virtues of a laundry product more powerful than dirt. By using the detergent, the power of the cleaning genie would be unleashed on the woman's laundry. Amazing! Yet the Bible says God's power is greater than anything on television.

answer

So, what does God's almighty power accomplish? The prophet Isaiah said by God's power a Prince of Peace will one day rule the world in righteousness and justice. God's power will bring a ruler to supremacy who will cause Jerusalem to be rebuilt and God's temple to be restored. And, Isaiah added, God's power will be evidenced in every word that God speaks. God's words will accomplish what He desires because God's power will bring it all to pass.

But there is more. The Bible proclaims God's almighty power over death. While the human body dies a little bit every day, the Gospels say God's power brought Lazarus back to life even after he had died and been buried for a few days. Hebrews declares God's power can transform the hurt of death, too, by bringing every spirit of every individual back into God's presence when time ends.

The Bible also says God's power will save and protect His children. The Psalms and the letters of the apostle Peter indicate God's children are delivered from their enemies and from the plans of Satan only through the power of God. The Gospels say God's saving power releases His children from the temptation to do wrong and cleanses their hearts from wickedness. In addition, many passages in both the Old and New Testaments provide illustrations of God's power protecting His children from wicked rulers, hungry lions, angry crowds, and violent storms. Indeed, God's power accomplishes much.

worth thinking about

▶ **God's power brings** about the changing of the seasons, the migration of birds and animals, and the movement of fish and whales in the sea.

▶ **God's power brings** about the miracle of birth from a tiny seed. One kernel of corn dropped into the dirt can yield hundred of kernels on a single ear—all because of God's power.

▶ **God's power can** restore the lives and fortunes of His people if they have suffered poverty, captivity, derision, or hurt.

God's power is exceeding, beyond our ability to conceive it. If we could only begin to comprehend—and access—God's power, everything about our lives would change for the better.

F. B. Meyer

question

What is an appropriate response to an all-powerful God?

The alarm clock goes off; you hit the snooze alarm button. You push past someone in a crowded aisle; you say, "Excuse me." Someone gives you a gift for your birthday; you show your gratitude with a note or a call. A restaurant server provides quick and accurate service; you leave a good tip. For many actions, there are appropriate, expected responses. So what is an appropriate response to the actions of an all-powerful God?

answer

The Bible discusses four responses to God. According to 2 Kings, an appropriate response to God is repentance. Think of it this way. As sunlight filters into a dirty room, it exposes cobwebs and dusty surfaces that need cleaning. Likewise, God's holiness shines a light of righteousness on the attitudes and actions of humanity. God's holiness illuminates all wrongdoing. The appropriate response to such illumination is repentance—a turning away from wrongdoing and turning toward God.

Another response to God derives from the first. According to Deuteronomy, when people have repented and turned from wrongdoing, the second appropriate response to God is obedience to His will and ways. God has given people written instructions in the Bible to serve as a guidebook to what God wants His children to do.

The third response to God is one that should come easily. The psalmist said the actions of almighty God should bring about joyful songs of praise. Worship is always an appropriate response to an all-powerful God.

The final response to God might not look like a response to God at all, but the Bible says it is. Paul's letter to the Ephesians says the loving response of people to one another is an appropriate response to God. What better response to God's love is there than for you to show kindness, love, and forgiveness to others?

worth thinking about

- ▶ **If people forget** to say thanks for a kindness, most societies consider such behavior inappropriate. Likewise, disobedience to God's ways is considered by the Bible an inappropriate response to almighty God.

- ▶ **According to Isaiah,** failing to respond to the actions of almighty God is considered an act of defiance, punishable by death.

- ▶ **The prophet Jeremiah** said false gods will not answer people, but when people turn to God, He will act in response to them with love, forgiveness, faithfulness, and grace.

> *Come, let us worship and bow down; let us kneel before the LORD our Maker. For He is our God, and we are the people of His pasture, the sheep under His care.*
>
> Psalm 95:6–7, HCSB

74

question

Is God always nearby?

A comedian once admitted his purchase of a new sports car sent his heart thrumming with the need for speed. On a quiet back street, he hit the gas and the car roared past seventy miles an hour. But in a split second, a police officer was pulling him over. The comedian was dumbfounded. He wondered where the cop had been. In his car's trunk? If the police were that handy, who also was close by all the time?

answer

The Bible can answer that question for you. God said, "Never will I leave you; never will I forsake you" (Hebrews 13:5, NIV). In the Gospels He promised, "Be sure of this: I am with you always, even to the end of the age" (Matthew 28:20, NLT). The Bible says God is always nearby.

After Moses died, the Israelites stood on the river's edge looking into the Promised Land. God had placed Joshua in charge of the people, yet Joshua was nervous. He knew it would not be easy to fill Moses' sandals. So in the first chapter of the Book of Joshua, God gave this young man a pep talk. He urged Joshua to be strong and courageous and to remember that God would always be with him. Four times in that short chapter God said, "I will be with you . . . I will never forsake you . . . I will go with you wherever you go!" What an assurance of God's presence.

But is God still nearby today? Indeed, He is! The Book of Exodus says God is always present with His people. He has promised to be present with His children at all times. Psalms says God is especially close to the poor, the widowed, and the needy. "The LORD is close to all who call on him, yes, to all who call on him in truth. He grants the desires of those who fear him, he hears their cries for help and rescues them" (Psalm 145:18–19, NLT). The Book of Isaiah resounds with the words that God is close to all who call on Him. Best of all, 1 Corinthians says God is as close as your heart, for God's Holy Spirit resides in the hearts of His children.

worth thinking about

▶ **The Bible says** God is far beyond the universe, yet present with His people at the same time. Hard to understand, but that is just how God is.

▶ **Though God** is always nearby, the Book of Job says God cannot be held, touched, or seen. He is Spirit and beyond the sensory reach of humanity.

▶ **The Bible says** God is near to those who do not follow Him, too. He leaves hints of His presence in creation so that everyone might seek and find Him.

> *There is nothing more important in any life than the constantly enjoyed presence of the Lord. There is nothing more vital, for without it we shall make mistakes.*
> Alan Redpath

question

Has anyone ever seen God?

One of the most popular tourist attractions in Hollywood is a bus tour that promises to go past movie stars' homes. The bus is always packed with camera-laden folks eager to catch a glimpse of someone famous. This same desire to see the unseeable has prompted the microscopic study of disease-causing germs and the construction of telescopes to view stars at the end of the universe. This same innate desire makes one wonder if God, too, can be seen.

answer

The opening chapters of the Bible reveal that Adam and Eve walked and talked with God face-to-face in the Garden of Eden. But as time passed, people chose to ignore God's standards. Their choices became increasingly selfish; their attitudes became more corrupt and less loving. So God separated Himself from people. Scripture indicates that God appeared to only a select few over the next millennia, mainly in dreams and visions. When Moses asked specifically to see God face-to-face, God refused, stating that humanity's perverseness was so bad any person would die instantly if they looked directly at God.

However, God still desired a personal, face-to-face relationship with humanity. Because of this, He chose to come to earth and live as a human being. The Bible says the folks who ate, worked, lived, and laughed with Jesus of Nazareth were eating, working, living, and laughing with God Himself. For more than thirty years, God once again lived among people. But as before, people chose to ignore Him and His ways. So God once again separated Himself from humanity. Because of humanity's willful wrongdoing, God has appeared in dreams and visions only to a few people over the last two thousand years.

Yet God has not given up on people. One day those who love God and do what His Word says will join Him in heaven. There they will see God face-to-face.

worth thinking about

▶ **The Bible says** that all people, good and evil, will see God face-to-face when time ends and His day of judgment comes.

▶ **While advertisers claim** that seeing is believing, the Bible says that in this world God's children must walk by faith and not by sight.

▶ **The visually impaired** use other senses to "see" the world around them. The Bible says you can see God through the eyes of faith, worship, and prayer.

> *God is not a distant, unknowable God. God has come near to us, has been among us. . . . May you experience hope and joy as you learn to see God in new ways.*
> Dale and Juanita Ryan

Is God always nearby?

If I flew on morning's wings to the
far western horizon, you'd find
me in a minute—you're
already there waiting!

Psalm 139:9–10, THE MESSAGE

76 question

How does God show His presence today?

The Old Testament tells the story of God's people living in slavery in Egypt. God sent plagues on the land of Egypt to convince the pharaoh to free the Israelite slaves. As the Israelites left Egypt, God Himself was with them in a pillar of cloud by day and a pillar of fire at night. This visible presence convinced all who saw it that God was with them. But how does God manifest His presence today?

answer

The Bible urges readers to look for and acknowledge God's presence in heaven and earth. Because God's glory—the revelation of His power and might—is visible throughout all creation, taking time to reflect on the wonders of creation helps keep God's presence in the forefront of a person's thoughts. God's presence was made visible when Jesus Christ walked on earth. That presence continues to be seen in the lives of those who love God and believe that Jesus died in their place so that God would forgive their sins. According to Philippians, believers who glorify Jesus Christ in their bodies also manifest God's presence to everyone around them.

God also uses His Holy Spirit today to shine a visible sign of His presence much like the pillar of cloud and fire shone in Exodus. John's Gospel says God's presence is seen today when His Holy Spirit convicts people of sin and wrongdoing. God's presence is also realized when His Spirit gives direction to believers and to the building up of the church. Paul's letter to the Philippians indicates that God's presence through the Holy Spirit is seen when prayers are offered and answered.

But God's presence is also seen in the changed lives of individuals. God shows His presence when He sends His blessings of fellowship among believers. He manifests His presence when freedom and peace are spoken between those who once opposed each other. And God's matchless presence is seen when His love is shared with all.

worth thinking about

▶ **The presence of God** is seen in the expression of joy. Joy is an aspect of God's Holy Spirit. Without God there would be no joy.

▶ **The presence of God** is seen through the activity of the gifts that the Holy Spirit gives to the church.

▶ **The Book of Acts** adds that God's presence is evident when encouragement flows from one individual to another.

> *Do not fear, for I am with you; do not be afraid, for I am your God. I will strengthen you; I will help you; I will hold on to you with My righteous right hand.*
> Isaiah 41:10, HCSB

question

Is God's Spirit in everyone?

Scientists say people are made up of a little salt, some minerals, and a lot of water. These common elements form the tissue, bone, and blood of every person on earth. Regardless of family background, race, or ethnic nationality, most human beings have the same number of bones, muscles, and internal organs. People are physically full of so many of the same things. But are folks spiritually full of the same things, too? Does God's Spirit live in everyone?

answer

According to the Bible, God's Spirit is present everywhere in the world. Although Genesis says human beings bear God's likeness in intellect and morals, the Bible clearly says only those who declare faith in God and accept God's gift of forgiveness can be filled with God's Spirit. Those who do not believe in God or follow His ways do not have God's Spirit in them. Instead, the prophet Isaiah said God's Spirit works outside these unbelievers, convicting them of wrongdoing and reminding them of God's presence, righteousness, and coming judgment.

Think of it this way. Even if your home has been wired with electricity, your kitchen will stay dark if you do not do something. You have to turn on the light switch to let electricity flow to the lightbulb so your kitchen can be flooded with light. In the same way, human beings have to do something to let "spiritual electricity" flow in and through their lives. Your heart is spiritually dark without God. But if you "flip the switch" by asking God's forgiveness and by making the choice to follow His ways, God's Spirit will fill you to overflowing. Your darkened heart will glow with all of God's Spirit, with all of His love, kindness, goodness, faith, joy, and peace. A heart filled with God's Spirit will experience assurance, freedom, wisdom, strength, inspiration, and divine power.

worth thinking about

▶ **According to the Bible**, those without God's Spirit living in them do not live godly lives. God's Spirit is the presence that gives people the desire to follow God's ways.

▶ **The Old Testament** records God's Spirit within people, too. Genesis notes God's Spirit was within Joseph, and Exodus says God's Spirit filled Bezalel and gave him skills needed to build God's tabernacle.

▶ **God's Spirit** is present in God's Son, Jesus. God's Spirit gives Jesus wisdom, understanding, counsel, might, and knowledge.

> *It is a blessed thing to be filled with the Spirit
> …to be filled with God's grace and heavenly
> benediction, to be filled with the fruits of
> righteousness, to be filled with the knowledge
> of His will. The heart is restless until it is full.*
>
> F. B. Meyer

78

Has God ever put His Spirit into an animal?

Coins go into a piggy bank. Clothes go into a suitcase. Feet slide into socks and shoes. Water courses over the tongue and down the throat, carrying the vitamins or medicines people ingest on a daily basis. That is what people do. They put things into other things. And God does that, too. He puts His Spirit into people so they may grow to be more like Him every day. But has God ever put His Spirit into an animal?

answer

Fairy tales and legends from other lands describe monsters inhabited by evil spirits. Some mystic religions also believe that spirits inhabit animals. But the Bible says otherwise. Though the serpent in Genesis 3 was able to speak and reason, nowhere does the Bible indicate the snake had a spirit. As Genesis narrates the story of Creation, it says human beings were the only ones given a spirit that was enlivened by God's breath. Several passages in the Bible indicate there are also spirits of the dead, but again, these are dead people, not dead animals. However, there are spirit beings at work in the world that are not human beings. Again, the Bible says these nonembodied spirits do not inhabit animals. The Book of James says nonembodied spirits serve God's purposes as tools of punishment or testing to inspire faith in God's people. According to the Gospels, evil spirits and demons exist without bodies, seeking to control or destroy God's children. Yet the Book of Revelation reminds readers that good spirits also exist and that Jesus Christ has been given victory over all spirits—good and evil.

So where do animals fit in the spirit picture? The Bible says that although animals never received God's Spirit, they have assisted God in His work. The serpent in Genesis spoke to Eve, a donkey in Numbers hollered at a prophet, and a great fish swallowed Jonah and carried him in its stomach for three days.

worth thinking about

▶ **The Bible indicates** evil spirits and demons may take on deformed animal shapes. Daniel dreamed of an evil leopard with wings and multiple heads, while several passages in Revelation refer to a "beast."

▶ **The Bible says** evil spirits have inhabited animals—with devastating consequences. Demons entered a herd of pigs and caused them to drown in a lake.

▶ **God's Spirit** within a person brings about good things. It is God's breath and Spirit in a person's life that bring wisdom and understanding.

> *Melt me. Mold me. Fill me, use me. Spirit of the Living God, fall fresh on me.*
> Daniel Iverson

question

If God is everywhere, why this emphasis on church?

The Bible says God is always present everywhere at the same time. He sees everything, knows everything, and controls everything. He is aware of His children's comings and goings. He always provides for the needs of His people. He promises to hear and respond every time His children speak to Him in prayer. And He keeps everything everywhere going according to His plan and purpose. So if God is everywhere and aware of everything, why all this emphasis on church?

answer

One of the first things God asked the Israelites to do as they left Egypt was to construct a tent that would be used as a meeting place for the people and God. Exodus provides a stirring account of the people's rejoicing as the presence of God settled over this meeting place for the first time. God created people with a need for relationship. This meeting place gave the Israelites a place to go to find relationship with God.

Likewise, the Bible says early Christians met together informally in homes, caves, and along hillsides to learn more about God, to join in corporate prayer and praise, to share His blessings with one another, and to enjoy fellowship with one another. Paul, Peter, and John taught that such meetings were necessary because the Christians were united to one Lord, filled with one Spirit, and committed to one gospel. Paul said they were like one body, bringing their abilities together so that each one could then receive what was needed for individual spiritual growth.

The church today operates on similar principles. Every member of a church is a necessary, vital part of a community of Christians, called out of the world to serve God. God chooses to use the church to be His hands to the world of love, joy, peace, and mercy. God wants the church to be a serving place.

worth thinking about

- ▶ **According to the Bible,** when services dismiss and folks head home, church is not over. The Bible says people do not just *go* to church; people *are* the church.

- ▶ **The Bible views church** as a corporate function, not something solitary. Watching a church service on television is okay, but it should not take the place of corporate worship.

- ▶ **God intends the church** to be alive and active—a body that praises and glorifies Him, that tells God's good news to everyone in the world, and that grows in understanding, character, and faith.

> *The church, you see, is not peripheral to the world; the world is peripheral to the church. The church is Christ's body, in which he speaks and acts, by which he fills everything with his presence.*
>
> Ephesians 1:23, THE MESSAGE

question

Does God love all people?

Nightly television news stories always have at least one bad guy—a robber, a terrorist, or a national leader who proclaims hatred of some person or group. The visual images that accompany this story are disturbing, often stirring up negative emotions. It is hard after viewing such stories to find love in your heart for such hurtful, mean-spirited people. Yet, does God love them? Does God love all people whether they are good or bad, lovable or unlovable?

answer

God may not condone their behavior, yet the Bible loudly proclaims that God does love all people. Matthew says God loves everyone and proves it by sending the rain on the just and the unjust, by giving sunlight to good people and wicked ones, too. Deuteronomy adds that God's love for the whole world is shown in His care for widows and orphans. Psalms says God loves all people and showers His compassion on everyone. And the Book of Acts indicates that God's love for the world is seen in plentiful harvests, good food, and joyful fellowship with friends.

But that is not all. God's nature is love—it is part of His character. So John says God proves His love for the world by giving people the gift of His Son. Ezekiel declares that God shows His love for everyone by extending His grace and mercy to those who have lived their lives in rebellion against Him. God gives life and breath to everyone and satisfies all needs because He loves the whole world.

However, the Bible also indicates God is especially committed to those who return His love and follow His ways. God's love for the world is deep and long-lasting, but His love for His children is a committed love, a sacrificial love, a loyal love that is eternally guaranteed by God's covenant and promises. God will always love everyone in the world, but He will save a spot beside His heavenly throne for those who love Him, too.

worth thinking about

▶ Because God's love is eternal, His love for the world is never-ending. According to Jeremiah, that endless love keeps pulling people's hearts toward God.

▶ Jesus said God's love for the world could be compared to a shepherd who left his flock to look for one lost sheep and kept looking until he found it.

▶ God loves the unlovable people of the world, but He does not endorse or condone their behavior. The Bible says God's children should love the unlovable as God loves them.

> God loved the world in this way: He gave His One and Only Son, so that everyone who believes in Him will not perish but have eternal life.
>
> John 3:16, HCSB

How big is God's love?

Jewelry advertisers seem to suggest giving a simple cubic zirconia ring will not really show how much you love someone. The ads indicate you have to do better. Better stones, bigger settings, and a velvet-lined box with the jeweler's name inscribed on it will truly demonstrate how big your love for another individual is. Since God does not give gifts of jewelry to His children, how can you tell how much He loves you? How big is God's love, anyway?

answer

▼

Love is the central aspect of God's character. Thus, the Bible says God's love is so big it is endless. Jeremiah says God's love is unfailing. The psalmist says God's love is from "everlasting to everlasting" (Psalm 103:17, NIV). And Isaiah adds God's love cannot be taken away and will never cease.

God's love is so big it pours out on people in wonderful ways, too. John says the gift of salvation through God's Son, Jesus, is a huge act of love. Ezekiel reminds readers that God's great love is seen in His loving actions toward those who are unlovable or cast out by others. And 2 Corinthians declares that God's love for His children is so big, He will act only in love toward them. His abundant love will always be more than enough for all their needs.

But that is not all. God's love is so big, the prophet Joel said it is lavishly extended to all people in the world regardless of race or nationality. The Psalms state God's vast stores of love are marked by His holiness and justice, too. His love is pure and always given freely and without partiality. And Deuteronomy proclaims that God's great big love is a covenant love, a contract that is unchangeable and cannot be withdrawn or canceled at any time.

So how big is God's love? The Bible says God's love is king-sized, for He is the King of all creation.

worth thinking about

▶ **God's love** is so big it encompasses His enemies. The Bible says God showed His great love for humanity by sending Christ to die for people while they were still God's enemies.

▶ **God's love** is so big nothing can stop it from reaching His children—not life, death, angels, demons, fears, worries, or even the powers of wickedness.

▶ **God's love** is so big it stretches out to help orphans and widows and provide food and clothing for a foreigner when no one else will.

The love of God is greater far than tongue or pen can ever tell; it goes beyond the highest star, and reaches to the lowest hell.

Frederick M. Lehman

question

▼

What is the love of God like?

After a day's work, it is nice to unwind in some comfortable clothes. Such an outfit may include a well-worn pair of pants that slip on without a struggle and a baggy shirt with an ages-old coffee stain. Topping off your ensemble might be a pair of shoes that have wear patterns in all the right places so there is no fear of blisters. When you slip into this getup, you can feel the stress melting away. Ah, such comfort!

answer

▼

In a way, God's love is like that comfortable, after-work getup. When God's love slips around you, it is more comfortable than a favorite pair of jeans, a well-aged shirt, or a shoe that does not cause blisters. God's love is a perfect fit for your life. In fact, the Bible says God's love is like that of a perfect Father, looking after the needs of His children at all times, teaching them to walk in His ways, and disciplining them when necessary. Jesus shared a story about an earthly father who welcomed a wayward son home, illustrating that God, too, longs for people to return to Him when they have wandered away.

The Book of Hosea also equates God's love for His children to that of an adoring husband who has made a covenant with a bride to love her exclusively, to gently lead and guide her and speak lovingly to her, and to enjoy a time of feasting and rejoicing together with her. Nothing is too good for this bride. Nothing is withheld. She is treasured, adorned with jewels, and smiled on with all of God's favor.

Truly, the Bible says the love of God is big, majestic, and immeasurable. Romans say God's love is a visible love, seen in the willingness of one person dying for another. God's love "is not jealous or boastful or proud or rude" (1 Corinthians 13:4–5, NLT). Welcoming. Comfortable. Restful. Kind. Indeed, that is what God's love is like.

worth thinking about

▶ **God's love** can be likened to the loyalty found between best friends. Best friends stick together in tough times and always care for each other. God's love is loyal like that, too.

▶ **God's love** is never suspicious, always hopeful in every circumstance, and full of protection to keep His children from grievous hurt.

▶ **God's love** is priceless and unquenchable. No one has enough wealth to buy God's love, and nothing can wash God's love away. Only He can give it away repeatedly.

What does it look like? It has hands to help others, feet to hasten to the poor and needy, eyes to see misery and want, ears to hear the sighs and sorrows of men. That is what love looks like.

Saint Augustine of Hippo

83 | question

How long will God's love last?

Purchasing a car is an important decision. In all probability, you would not purchase an automobile without first asking friends who own this type of vehicle or consumer advocacy groups for information about the reliability and longevity of the car. In the same way, making a lifetime spiritual commitment to God is an important decision. You might wonder about the longevity of God's care for you. How long will God's love last, anyway? Is it reliable no matter what?

answer

No extended warranties are needed when it comes to God's love, for the Bible says God's love will never end. His love will last longer than time. Jeremiah says God's love is an everlasting love that constantly draws people back to God. John adds that because God's nature is love itself, His love will last as long as God does. Hebrews says God existed before time and will continue to exist after time ends; therefore, God's love will continue unabated forever.

The psalmist recognized this eternal, everlasting facet of God's love when he penned Psalm 136—a musical reminder to worshipers of God's love. Every other line in each of the twenty-six verses repeats, "His love endures forever" (NIV). The prophet Isaiah expanded this theme as he revealed God's words to His people. God acknowledges there might be times when His anger with human willfulness might cause Him to turn away for a moment. But God assures His people that even if the mountains and hills collapse under multiple earthquakes, His unfailing love will not be shaken, because God will always have compassion on His children and continue to love them.

Indeed, God's love will last your whole life through—and beyond. Some mothers can walk away from their children and stop loving them, but God will never do that. Why? God writes His children's names on the palm of His hand. He will never forget you or ever stop loving you.

worth thinking about

▶ **God's love** for those who love and respect Him will continue forever. As an added benefit, God's goodness will continue on to their grandchildren, too.

▶ **God's eternal love** is manifested in His children. God's Holy Spirit pours God's continual, steadfast, practical love into God's children and through them toward others.

▶ **The Book of Colossians** says God's endless love motivates and inspires His children to live for Him instead of for themselves.

> *I have loved you, my people, with an everlasting love. With unfailing love I have drawn you to myself.*
> Jeremiah 31:3, NLT

question

How does God show His love?

People give gifts at holidays and birthdays to show someone how much they are loved by another. To convey the same message, other people perform tasks they know will be appreciated. Still others show their love by spending time together, sending a note of affection, or enfolding another person in a big hug. Since God is not physically present today to confirm His love in these ways, how does He show His love to people?

answer

If you look between the lines of life, you can see God's love all around you. God's love causes the earth to orbit the sun to receive even heating and cooling. God's love makes the moon pull tides in to the shore, bringing weather patterns along that provide rain for the crops people grow. God's love stimulates tree leaves to absorb carbon dioxide and release oxygen. The Bible says all of these scientifically observed occurrences happen because God loves people. God knows humanity needs these things to survive, so God set these things in motion and keeps them going so people can live.

The Bible also says God's love was shown when He became human. Since humanity's failings required a cure for wrongdoing, the Book of Romans says God showed His love for people by giving His Son as the remedy for sin. The Bible says there is no greater love than dying for someone else. Paul reminded the Ephesians that God's love is demonstrated in His kindness, grace, and forgiveness. And 1 Timothy says God's love prompts Him to offer people eternal life as His children.

God also shows His love by giving you something tangible of Himself. When Jesus was on earth, folks could touch God and feel His embrace. You may not be able to touch God today and get a hug, but He has given you something to prove His love for you—a love letter written in His own words. That love letter is the Bible.

worth thinking about

▶ **Love can be defined** as unselfish concern about another's welfare. God shows this aspect of His love by answering prayer, by judging justly, and by showering His blessings on people.

▶ **God's love** for people cannot be separated from His holiness. Therefore, God shows His love for people by making a way for them to be as righteous as He is.

▶ **God shows** His love for people by being their model for human love. By observing and imitating God's love, people can better love one another.

Jesus is the channel through which the life and love of God reach us, that we may pass them on in loving ministry, and in so doing we create and store up for ourselves infinite joy.

F. B. Meyer

question

▼

Why does God love people so much?

Why do people have belly buttons? Why do kittens have fur? Toddlers often ask such "Why?" questions to help quantify their surroundings. Sometimes the answers are simple and easily verbalized. But many times a "Why?" question leads to a host of others that cannot be answered easily because the concepts are beyond the child's understanding. Adults often ask "Why?" questions, too, to help quantify God. For example, folks sometimes feel the need to know why God loves people so much.

answer

▼

The complete answer to why God loves people so much is beyond human comprehension. In fact, the Bible never gives the "why" behind God's everlasting love for people. Rather, the Bible takes God's love for people for granted. However, by piecing together what you know of God and His written Word, you can draw conclusions that help answer this question a bit.

For example, Genesis says after God created the first man it became apparent he had no companion in life. As the man slept, God used a rib from the man and created the first woman to be the man's helper. In the New Testament, Jesus once heard the teachers of the law gossiping about His habit of eating with sinners. Jesus reminded the teachers, "It is not the healthy who need a doctor, but the sick" (Mark 2:17, NIV). When God created humanity, people were made in God's image but on a lower level than angels and other heavenly beings. So what do these passages have to do with God's love?

All three passages point out the neediness of humanity. People do not possess angelic powers. They have bodies that sicken and die. They need other people around to function well. The conclusion you can draw from these passages is that God knew people's needs and felt love and compassion for them. So one conclusion you can draw from the Bible about why God loves people so much is because people need it.

worth thinking about

▶ **In the Psalms,** David clearly asks God why He cares for people, but David never receives a clear answer, just an assurance that God loves.

▶ **The Bible teaches** that every person born since Adam and Eve has the mark of sin. God's love is the only means people have to be made sinless.

▶ **Only human beings** will ever know God's love. While God cares about what happens to plants, animals, and angels, John 3:16 says His love is reserved for humanity.

> *When the goodness and love for man appeared*
> *from God our Savior, He saved us—not by*
> *works of righteousness that we had done,*
> *but according to His mercy.*
> Titus 3:4–5, HCSB

How big is God's love?

Your roots will grow down into God's love and keep you strong. And may you have the power to understand, as all God's people should, how wide, how long, how high, and how deep his love is.

Ephesians 3:17–18, NLT

86 question

How does God's love affect human love?

While most digital cameras reveal the photograph just taken in a view screen on the camera, film cameras depend upon a developing process to expose the image that has been imprinted on the negative. Only when the film has been bathed in chemicals in a darkroom does a picture emerge. In the same way, when God's love washes over a human heart, a godly picture of love emerges, for God's love affects human love in many ways.

answer

Love—that caring commitment toward self and others—is grounded in God's nature. By His words, actions, and attitudes, God clearly shows what love is and delineates the course of human love. According to the Bible, human love is to be patterned after God's love for His people. Since God's love is seen in His actions toward His children, human love needs to be others-oriented, too. The letters of John in the New Testament say God's children will reflect His love when they perform loving deeds for other people.

God's love is also the catalyst for human love when it gives itself sacrificially. The Book of Galatians states God's sacrificial giving of His Son to the world is the example God's children should follow when they give of their time, resources, and talents. Proverbs indicates God's children should love as God does and be loyal like He is, too.

Human love within the family is also affected by God's love. The Book of Numbers says God's love for home and country should pour from the hearts of His children. Proverbs reminds parents to love their children as God loves His children. The apostle Paul's letter to the Ephesians says spouses should care for each other as God cares for His bride, the church. Indeed, God's love should make such an impact on His children's lives that they will reflect His love to every person in every situation.

worth thinking about

▶ **God's love** affects human love in the outpouring of care and concern for the sick. Paul's converts in Galatia were not put off by his illness, but rather showered him with God's love.

▶ **John says** God's love affects human love when people reach out to help those with material needs just as God reaches out in love to meet your needs.

▶ **The Book of Acts** says God's love is reflected in the way people greet one another with hugs, kisses, and weeping. God's love makes these greetings both possible and acceptable.

> If we have got the true love of God shed abroad in our hearts, we will show it in our lives. We will not have to go up and down the earth proclaiming it. We will show it in everything we say or do.
>
> Dwight Lyman Moody

87

question

Will God stop loving people if they are bad?

Picture this. Two grade-school children have a disagreement over the rules of a pickup football game. The disagreement is not resolved to the satisfaction of the owner of the football, so the ball and the owner quit the game and head for home. The question is, is God like that? Will He ever quit what He has started? He wants people to be good and kind, but will He quit loving them if they are bad?

answer

God cannot stop loving, no matter what, because the Bible says God's person is made up of love. But the Bible does indicate God can be disappointed with humanity's bad behavior. The Book of Judges chronicles such actions of people and God.

According to Judges, when Joshua died after serving as the second person in charge of Israel, there was no one to serve as Israel's leader. As a result, God's people began to fall away from following God. They compromised with their enemies. They began to worship the false gods of nearby nations. Despite their behavior, God still loved His people. He even sent His angel to urge the people to turn away from their wrongdoing. Fifteen times in the Book of Judges, God's people turned away from Him, and fifteen times God sent a wake-up call to the people to turn back to Him. God's people suffered severely for their poor choices, and it took a long time for them to turn back to God. But despite their stubbornness, God never stopped loving them.

When the Jews returned to the Promised Land after a long captivity in Babylon, Nehemiah reminded the returnees of the bad behavior of their ancestors as recorded in Judges. Nehemiah also reminded the people that God did not desert them because God is "gracious and compassionate, slow to anger and abounding in love" (Nehemiah 9:17, NIV). While God is not pleased with wrongdoing, He will never stop loving His children.

worth thinking about

▶ **God is patient** with those who do wrong and is willing to forgive them, but He will not leave the guilty unpunished. He loves them enough to correct them.

▶ **If it were not for** God's loving hand extended toward sinners, no one would survive. He offers love and forgiveness to all.

▶ **Even if** your parents and grandparents turned away from God, you can always come to Him and He will pour His love out on you.

> *There is tremendous relief in knowing that His love is utterly realistic, based at every point on prior knowledge of the worst about me, so that no discovery now can disillusion Him about me.*
>
> J. I. Packer

88

How is God's love reflected through His Son, Jesus?

Artists use different techniques to give depth and perspective to their paintings. Sometimes an artist will add a pond to a painting to reflect the amount of light coming onto the canvas. This technique of reflection also enlarges the overall view of the painting, giving the eye much more to see. God's love is so big it is hard to see it all at once, too. So God reflects His love through His Son, Jesus, to show His love more clearly.

answer

While Jesus was alive on earth, He reflected God's love in everything He said and did. Paul's second letter to the Corinthians states that God's love prompted Jesus to leave heaven and come to earth as a person. The Gospels declare that God's love stirred Jesus to reach out with love and compassion to selfish, willful people. And 2 Thessalonians adds that even now Jesus loves all the children of God because God loves them first.

The Gospels say Jesus also reflected God's love to those around Him by showing compassion to the poor and needy, by loving and accepting little children, and by showing care and concern for the welfare of those who followed Him. God's love is also reflected in Jesus' obedience to do whatever God wanted Him to do. Mark and Luke recorded Jesus' prayerful struggle in the Garden of Gethsemane. God's amazing love for all people meant a horrific death sentence for Jesus. Yet He was obedient to God's plan. The Bible says Jesus reflected God's love for humanity by dying for others on the cross.

God's love is also reflected through Jesus in every child of God. God's love is the spark that motivates God's children to follow Jesus' teachings. His total giving of Himself to others inspires God's children to give of themselves to others, too. And the Book of Romans says as Jesus' love abides in the hearts of God's children, God's love is poured out and reflected to all.

worth thinking about

▶ God's love for the family was reflected by Jesus' love for His family. One of Jesus' last wishes was that His mother would be taken care of by His disciples.

▶ God's love and concern for those who could not care for themselves was reflected by Jesus' miracles— feeding the hungry, healing the sick, and giving sight to the blind.

▶ God's love and compassion for the bereaved and burdened was reflected by Jesus' raising the dead and giving rest to the weary.

> *Christ was without sin, but for our sake God made him share our sin in order that in union with him we might share the righteousness of God*
>
> 2 Corinthians 5:21, GNT

question

▼

What does God give to those whom He loves?

If you love a pet, you might purchase a special toy for it to play with. If you love a favorite food, you might stock your refrigerator or pantry with enough of that item so you will never run out. If you love an individual, you might give an expensive present like a diamond ring or a set of golf clubs to show how much you care. But what does God give to those whom He loves?

answer

▼

God gives many gifts to the people He loves. John's Gospel says the greatest gift God gives the world is His only Son, Jesus. According to Hebrews, Jesus is God's payment to buy humanity back from a destiny in hell. Because God gave this wonderful gift, the Book of Ephesians says people can become children of God with all the royal rights and privileges of heaven. And Hebrews adds two more gifts: Jesus becomes a heavenly big brother and people gain easy access to God's throne room through prayer.

Though those are wonderful gifts in themselves, God does not stop there. To those whom He loves, God promises a life that is transformed, a hope of future glory, and a promise that everything will work out for good. The Book of Romans declares that God gives the gift of eternal life to those He loves. Paul's letters to the early churches say God also gives spiritual gifts, talents, and abilities to those He loves, and Peter adds that these gifts come with an extra measure of God's grace.

God gives other gifts, too. The Book of Acts reminds readers that God bestows His Holy Spirit on His children. Luke's Gospel says God sometimes gifts those He loves with children. James indicates God gives wisdom to those He loves, while Ecclesiastes says God grants job satisfaction, too. God graciously gives all things to those whom He loves. What wonderful gifts from a wonderful God.

worth thinking about

▶ **Because of God's** great love for people, He mercifully "made us alive with Christ even when we were dead in transgressions" (Ephesians 2:5, NIV).

▶ **God gives good** things to those whom He loves. He has stored these good things up in heaven and gives them openly to His children.

▶ **For those who** love God, He will help them grasp how wide, long, high, and deep His love is in return.

You called, you cried, you shattered my deafness, you sparkled, you blazed, you drove away my blindness, you shed your fragrance, and I drew in my breath, and I pant for you.

Saint Augustine of Hippo

question
▼
Where did God come from?

A little goldfish, his siblings, and cousins swam together in the tank at the pet store. One day a net dropped into the tank and scooped the little fish into a plastic bag. Soon the little fish was spilled out into a glass fishbowl, far from his siblings and cousins. As he looked up to the top of the fishbowl, he saw two people and wondered where they came from. People sometimes wonder goldfish-type questions, too.

answer
▼

Though people are bigger and smarter than goldfish, they may look up at God and wonder where He came from. Such a query is a goldfish-in-a-fishbowl type of question. In the goldfish story, the people existed long before the goldfish ever spilled out into the fishbowl. The fish only became aware of the people when the fish was brought into their home, their sphere of influence, their time and space. Because a goldfish has a short life span, it is most likely the people were there in their place even before the goldfish was born. So, for the goldfish to wonder where the people came from is a bit hard to answer. The people had always been there; it was the goldfish that was new to the surroundings.

The same rationale applies when people wonder about where God came from. According to the Bible, God has always existed. People are the ones who move in and out of time and space as they live and die. People are the ones in the fishbowl suddenly aware of God's presence. The Psalms say God existed before the world was created. He existed before time began and will continue to exist after time ends. The Bible says God is.

Yet, where did He come from? No one knows. Just as the goldfish never knew where the people came from, so people do not know where God came from, either.

worth thinking about

▶ **Children sometimes ask,** "Where do babies come from?" Depending on the child, parents may divulge more or less information to answer the question. Likewise, God wisely grants and withholds information about Himself, too.

▶ **Jeremiah suggests** if people want to find God's home place, they should study the road map of God's Word. Much is hidden within the Bible; and much will be revealed to those who search diligently.

▶ **Isaiah says** God inhabits the heavens, and Job indicates that this heavenly realm is somewhere other than on earth. Yet the Bible is silent about God's whereabouts before time began.

> *Your throne, O LORD, has stood from time immemorial. You yourself are from the everlasting past.*
> Psalm 93:2, NLT

91

▾
Where does God live?

If you hear someone speaking with an accent different from your own, you might ask where that person comes from. Wanting to know where people live is a connecting point, because your home is the place where you belong. If asked that question, you might answer in global terms by telling people what country you come from. Or you might convey the specific details of your street address. But what about God? Where does God live?

answer

▾

When Jesus taught His disciples about prayer, He instructed them to address God as their Father in heaven. Why? Deuteronomy says heaven is the place where God dwells. The Book of Revelation adds that God shares His heavenly home with His angels. And Ecclesiastes declares God's heavenly home is also His vantage point to oversee the world.

Yet God's home is not limited to heaven. Exodus describes in detail a Tent of Meeting that God instructed Moses and the ancient Israelites to build so that God could live with them in the Sinai Desert. When the Israelites camped and put up the Tent of Meeting, God's Spirit would come like a cloud and fill the inner room of the tent. After Israel finally made its home in the Promised Land, King David amassed lumber, stones, and gold to build a permanent temple for God in Jerusalem. As the temple was dedicated, David's son Solomon acknowledged that even the highest heaven cannot contain God, much less a man-made temple. But God's Spirit, like a cloud, came down and filled the inner room of the temple so God's presence would be with His people once again.

And God has established another home for Himself, too. The Book of Acts says God's home is now on earth. He lives within the hearts of His children through the presence of His Holy Spirit. Hard to comprehend, but the Bible says it is true. Both heaven and hearts are homes for God.

worth thinking about

▶ **Since Jesus** paid for humanity's sins, God's home is now, in part, present with God's children on earth whenever they obey God's commands.

▶ **God is also** at home wherever His grace is revealed. For example, if God's unmerited favor is seen in a person who used to do wrong but now does right, then God is at home in that person.

▶ **The Bible says** God does not live in man-made temples. He is not bound by one address. He lives wherever He chooses because He is present everywhere all at the same time.

> *No one has ever seen God. But if we love each other, God lives in us, and his love is brought to full expression in us.*
> 1 John 4:12, NLT

92

Can God be found by people?

In a scavenger hunt, people are given a specific locale and a limited time to acquire a list of items. With hard work and quick searching the items can be found, sometimes in unusual locations. In the same way, people can look for spiritual things and find them in unexpected places, too. The Bible says God can be found by people if they look in the right way and in the right places. So how can people find God?

answer

The best way for people to find God is to read the Bible and pray. The Book of Deuteronomy promises if you seek God, you will find Him if you look for Him with all your heart. Matthew says you must ask, seek, and knock in order to receive, find, and discover. Indeed, the Bible declares, "Stand at the crossroads and look; ask for the ancient paths, ask where the good way is, and walk in it" (Jeremiah 6:16, NIV).

Some folks in Bible times found God in dreams. Daniel and Isaiah saw visions of God on His throne, whereas John saw God in the new, holy city of Jerusalem. Others found God in the world around them, finding traces of God in the things of creation. Job says you can find hints of God's presence in the wind, the oceans, and the weather patterns. Matthew tells the story of some kings who recognized a star in the sky as being the beacon to bring them to God the Son at Bethlehem.

Many people find God in their daily circumstances, too. For example, when there is more month than money and God's child asks for help, God may not make a visible appearance, but His presence will be felt as the bills get paid. When seeking God, remember, you will find Him only if you really want to. It might take some work, but God promises He will let you find Him.

worth thinking about

▶ **Paul reminded readers** that the Jews had trouble finding God because they were looking for Him through works, not faith.

▶ **The Bible says** some will find God in dreams and visions, but most people will find God in the ordinary occurrences of daily life as God provides, guides, and protects.

▶ **God will sometimes** reveal Himself to those who do not seek Him. For example, God appeared to Abram in the city of Ur and told him to leave his home and follow God.

> *I will be found of you. God has said it, and we may depend upon it; seek and you shall find.*
> Matthew Henry

93

question

Is God ever coming back to earth?

Radio Bible teacher Vance Havner once said, "When God splits the skies and the stars fall, the moon turns to blood and men cry for rocks and mountains to fall on them, it's going to be pretty hard for some of us to keep from saying, 'I told you so.'" To what was this Bible teacher referring, you may ask? He was speaking about what Bible scholars call the Second Coming—God's return to earth when time ends.

answer

Indeed, the Bible says God will come back to earth—but not as a baby in a manger, an itinerant preacher in the Middle East, or a bruised body on a hillside cross. God will return in the recognizable, human body form of Jesus. He will come at the end of time to raise the dead, judge the world, and destroy all opposition to God.

When will all this happen? Jesus said, "No one knows about that day or hour, not even the angels in heaven, nor the Son, but only the Father" (Matthew 24:36, NIV). Just as people in the days of Noah did not know when the rains were going to come, so no one will know when God will return to earth.

Yet the Bible does give some indication of things that will happen as God gets ready to come back. The Book of Revelation says the sun will go dark, the moon will cease to shine, and stars will fall out of the sky. The oceans will be tossed about and cause destruction. As this happens, Matthew's Gospel says the sky will be pulled back and Jesus will come out of heaven in the clouds. The whole world will be able to see Him. He will step onto the Mount of Olives in Jerusalem and the earth will shake. But until that marvelous day, God's children are to look to the skies as the early church did and joyfully anticipate God's promised return.

worth thinking about

▶ **The Bible is full** of promises about the return or second coming of Jesus. Seventeen Old Testament books and twenty-three books of the New Testament give special emphasis to this great event.

▶ **Much of the Bible** speaks about the future. For every prophecy written in the Bible about the first coming of God to earth, there are eight about His return to earth at the end of time.

▶ **Paul urges** God's children to be watchful for God's return. No one knows the exact time this will occur, but it will be a glorious day.

> *The early Christians were looking not for a cleft in the ground called a grave but for a cleavage in the sky called Glory.*
> Alexander MacLaren

question

How could a holy God create evil?

Every culture or society in the world has some concept of an evil being, invisible to the eye yet active in lives and situations. But where did such a being come from? According to Genesis, God created everything on earth, in the sea, in the skies, and in the heavens. The Bible also says God is holy, with no tendency toward wrongdoing. Since good and evil are opposites, how could a holy God create evil?

answer

After God created everything, the first chapter of the Bible says He looked around and declared everything was very good. Yet before God made the world, the Book of Job says God had already created the angels. And the prophet Isaiah said bad things were happening in heaven even as God was finishing the creation of the world.

According to Isaiah, Satan was the most beautiful of God's created angels. He was an archangel with access to the holiest places in heaven and to the Garden of Eden, too. The Bible says Satan was sinless on the day he was created.

Yet God did not create angels and people as robots forced to love Him, but rather as beings with the capacity to choose. Angels and people can choose to love God

or not, to follow God's ways or go their own way. God did not create the evil in Satan. Rather, Satan saw his beauty and status and said, "I will make myself like the Most High" (Isaiah 14:14, NIV). Satan chose to covet God's high position over everything. He chose to be proud and do things his way instead of God's way. The Bible says those choices are evil and sinful. Since God is holy and cannot live with sinfulness, the Book of Revelation says God turned Satan out of heaven and cast him to earth where he has been tempting people to sin ever since. God never created evil; Satan chose it. Unfortunately, people sometimes choose it, too.

worth thinking about

▶ **God allows evil** in this world because He can bring good out of it. He is the God of redemption, waiting for people to turn away from wrong and turn toward righteousness.

▶ **Genesis says** all people—good and bad—have some of God's image. Even a tiny bit of God's image limits the scope of evil. Without such limits, the earth and its inhabitants would be destroyed.

▶ **The job of conquering** evil is not hopeless because God is stronger than evil itself. With His help, God's children can resist evil and conquer it, too.

We are too Christian really to enjoy sinning, and too fond of sinning really to enjoy Christianity. Most of us know perfectly well what we ought to do; our trouble is that we do not want to do it.

Peter Marshall

question

What does God's voice sound like?

Cell phone ring tones and telephones with caller ID can help identify incoming telephone calls. But sometimes a telephone call will ring through with an unfamiliar number. When you answer such a call, you have to wait for the individual on the other end to speak so you can identify the caller. You hear a few words and know it is a friend or family member by the sound of his or her voice. But what does God's voice sound like?

answer

You will never get a telephone call from God, yet the Bible says God does communicate with His children. In fact, God speaks in many different ways. The Book of Job suggests God's voice resounds in the rushing, mighty winds, the rumbling and rolling of thunder, and the cascading noisiness of waves and waterfalls. Yet 1 Kings says Elijah heard roaring fire and rushing wind when God came to him, but God's voice was still and small, like a whisper.

Many Bible characters audibly heard God's voice in dreams and visions. The Gospels say God spoke audibly for crowds to hear, too, when Jesus was baptized in the Jordan River. The Book of Ephesians says God's children may hear God's voice like an inner echo directing their decisions. John's Gospel says sheep hear a shepherd giving commands from behind them as they walk through a pasture. God's children are like those sheep, recognizing the voice of their heavenly Shepherd when He nudges them to do or say something or to go somewhere.

In addition, the Book of Deuteronomy proclaims that God's voice is awe-inspiring. And, if you are in doubt that He is speaking to you, Matthew says you should ask God to confirm His voice in an unmistakable way. John says God's voice will bring you closer to Him. Exodus declares God's voice will prompt you to live in obedience to His commands. Indeed, the Bible promises that as you get to know God better, you will easily recognize His voice whenever He speaks.

worth thinking about

▶ A person's voice can be a guide to his or her character. The Bible says a false witness "pours out lies" (Proverbs 6:19, NIV).

▶ A person's voice can influence people to do irrational things—Hitler stirred thousands to kill Jews. God's voice influences people to do things, too, but His directives are good.

▶ A person's voice may continue for too long "like a constant dripping" (Proverbs 19:13, NIV). However, God's voice is heard when it is needed and for as long as needed.

> *I saw the glory of the God of Israel coming from the east. His voice sounded like the roar of mighty waters, and the earth shone with His glory.*
> Ezekiel 43:2, HCSB

question

Where does God live?

answer

The world is unable to receive Him because it doesn't see Him or know Him. But you do know Him, because He remains with you and will be in you.

John 14:17, HCSB

question

How does God speak to people today?

A century ago, people depended on print media such as magazines and newspapers to keep them up to date on current events. Handwritten letters kept families and friends apprised of personal happenings. The telegraph helped speed communication then, too, and the invention of the telephone was considered a modern marvel. Today people communicate at the speed of light—on cell phones, the Internet, and with instant-messaging. But how does God speak to people today?

answer

A contemporary Christian song poetically acknowledged there's no way to write God a letter or call Him on the phone. There's no way to visit Him at His home or a coffee shop. Yet the Bible says God's children can talk with God any time and hear from Him, too. How?

During Old Testament times, God often spoke to individuals through visions. Abraham, Joseph, Jacob, and Daniel experienced this type of communication with God. When Jesus came to earth, God modified His communication style and opened a more direct path for His children to dialogue with Him. The Bible says God placed His Holy Spirit within the spirits of His children on the Day of Pentecost. Since that time, God has been directly communicating His wishes to His children through the Holy Spirit. What some folks call a conscience might be God's Spirit influencing them to choose to do good things. What other people sense as a nudge might be God urging them to be His agents of love.

God speaks today through the pages of the Bible, too. Paul reminded Timothy that God inspired every word in the Bible so Scripture is "useful to teach us what is true and to make us realize what is wrong in our lives. It corrects us when we are wrong and teaches us to do what is right. God uses it to prepare and equip his people to do every good work" (2 Timothy 3:16–17, NLT).

worth thinking about

▶ **According to** 2 Peter, the first-century apostles heard from God through dreams and visions. God sometimes uses such miracles today to speak to His children, too.

▶ **Prayer is another** avenue of communication with God. The prophet Amos reminded readers that God listens to His children when they pray and responds in ways they can recognize.

▶ **The life Jesus** lived on this earth is a visible means of God's communication with people, too. By studying what Jesus said and how He lived, people can understand how He wants them to live today.

> *In the past God spoke to our ancestors many times and in many ways through the prophets, but in these last days he has spoken to us through his Son.*
> Hebrews 1:1–2, GNT

97

question
▼

Can God be known and completely understood?

No matter how well you know someone, chances are you can still be surprised by an action, attitude, or turn of a phrase you might not have heard or known before. Those unexpected surprises keep your relationship fresh and interesting. In the same way, your faith relationship with God stays fresh and interesting as you continue to get to know Him. But will you ever be able to really know God and completely understand Him?

answer
▼

People can gain some understanding about God through various means. Hebrews says faith brings about an understanding of God, while the Psalms add the Bible is another source of knowledge about God. The Book of Job states that God's Holy Spirit enlightens the understanding of God's children to the ways of God. And the Book of Proverbs suggests that people can find additional meaning and discernment about God through wise teaching.

Folks can also get to know God through His actions and dealings with His people. The accounts in 1 Kings give God's children an understanding of the way God delivers His people. The Book of Exodus shares narratives that help people know how God provides and cares for His children, while the Book of Numbers says God judges His people but also restores them. By observing such acts, people can understand and get to know God better. Yet Daniel adds that only as God reveals Himself to His children can people really get to know and understand Him better.

Human minds and understanding are limited. People cannot comprehend everything about God. But God's children are assured that one day the eyes of their understanding will be opened. When God's children enter heaven, they will finally be able to know God in His fullness. What a day that will be!

worth thinking about

▶ **When a person** turns from wrongdoing and accepts God's offer of forgiveness through Jesus' death for sin, the experience of Jesus' living in and through an individual reveals knowledge of God that is not found in any other way.

▶ **The Bible says** knowing facts about God is not satisfying. A faith in God that is significant, profitable, and satisfying is a faith that is personal and rooted in your heart.

▶ **One day people** will not have to have teachers tell them about God. People will be able to know God because God will be their teacher.

> *Since it is God we are speaking of, you do not understand it. If you could understand it, it would not be God.*
> Saint Augustine of Hippo

question

▼

Does God listen when people talk to Him?

A television commercial focused on a couple in their living room. She had just purchased a new dress. He was reading the sports scores in the newspaper. As the wife modeled her dress, she asked, "Does this outfit make me look fat?" Without even looking up from his paper, the husband replied, "You betcha!" Advertisers know people do not do a very good job of paying attention and listening to one another. But does God listen when people talk to Him?

 **answer**

▼

Does God listen? You betcha! The Bible says God listens even when people *are not* speaking directly *to* Him. God is present everywhere at all times. He hears everything that is going on all over the world at the same time. However, what God hears is not just white noise. Every word spoken is heard and paid attention to.

Consider this. When Miriam and Aaron stood in the Sinai wilderness gossiping and complaining against Moses, the Bible says God heard them and struck Miriam with leprosy. As the Israelites wandered through the wilderness, they began to grumble about not having any meat to eat. The Book of Numbers says God heard this protest, too, and provided quail for the complaining people. When the twelve spies Moses sent into the Promised Land returned to give their report to the people, God heard their faithless comments. The unbelief of ten of the spies made God so angry He swore they would never enter the Promised Land.

God hears other things, too. The Book of Genesis says that Leah, the first wife of Jacob, was not as loved as Jacob's second wife, Rachel. When Leah gave birth to her second son, she named him Simeon, which means "hearing." Leah rejoiced, saying, "Because the LORD heard that I am not loved, he gave me this one too" (Genesis 29:33, NIV). God also hears the praises of His people as they worship.

worth thinking about

▶ **According to Luke's** Gospel, when two disciples headed toward Emmaus, they talked together about Jesus. He miraculously appeared and joined their conversation, knowing what they were discussing without even asking.

▶ **The Book of Deuteronomy** indicates God heard the voices of the ancient Israelites as they groaned under the oppression of their Egyptian slave masters.

▶ **God hears** those who continue in wrongdoing, saying, "I have listened attentively, but they do not say what is right. No one repents of his wickedness" (Jeremiah 8:6, NIV).

> *Be the conference ever so private, God sees and hears in secret and will reward openly.*
> Matthew Henry

question

Does God answer every prayer?

A Hollywood blockbuster once explored the concept of answered prayer by picturing what would happen if an ordinary man were given godlike powers. At one point, the film showed the fellow awakening to an e-mail in-box crammed with millions of prayer requests. When the man finally relinquished his special powers, he acknowledged God's greater wisdom in knowing how to best answer the world's prayers. But does God really answer every prayer that everyone in the world prays?

answer

Scripture indicates that God is a prayer-answering God. He promises to hear and respond to His children's requests because prayer is God's communication lifeline with His children. Prayer offers God's people a means of seeking God's guidance and will for their lives. As God's will is lived out in their lives, God receives glory and honor.

The Bible assures you throughout its pages that God hears the prayers of those who are humble in heart. The Book of Proverbs says God's ear is attentive to those who are righteous and obedient to God. The prophet Jeremiah also reminded readers that God listens to the prayers of those who are single-minded in following

God alone. And each one of the Gospels resounds with Jesus' assurance that God hears His children who pray in faith believing that God will answer.

But even though God is in the prayer-answering business, He does not answer every prayer that is prayed. God does not respond to the prayers of those who do wrong. The apostle Peter declared that any unconfessed sin or wrongdoing will keep God from hearing a prayer—even a prayer from one of God's children. James added that selfishness and a lack of faith can also keep God from answering prayer. The prophet Zechariah reminded readers that acts of injustice or disobedience to God's will and ways will keep prayers from being answered, too.

worth thinking about

▶ According to 1 John, God willingly answers those prayers that agree with God's will because the Holy Spirit helps God's children pray for those things that are in God's will.

▶ God promises to hear the prayers of His children in need and to start working on the answer before the prayer is finished.

▶ Though God does not respond to the prayers of the wicked for rescue, blessing, healing, or aid, He will respond to their prayers for mercy and forgiveness.

> If our conscience does not condemn us, we have courage in God's presence. We receive from him whatever we ask, because we obey his commands and do what pleases him.
>
> 1 John 3:21–22, GNT

100 question

Does God have questions for humanity?

Folks come to faith with lots of questions. When bad things happen, people ask God why. They wonder what God is doing when a tsunami claims a whole society. When your prayers are seemingly unanswered for days on end you might wonder where God is. Is He listening? Does He care? When will He take care of things? You have questions. Lots of them. But what about God? Does God ever have questions for people?

answer

Indeed He does. God has many questions for people. In the Book of Genesis, God called out to Adam and asked, "Where are you?" after Adam had eaten what God had forbidden. Because God knows everything, God already knew Adam had done wrong. And God already knew where Adam was. God's question was not to help locate Adam. It was meant to start a conversation so Adam could confess what he had done. In the same way, God asked Cain where his brother, Abel was. God knew Cain had murdered his brother. The ground was covered with Abel's blood. But God questioned Cain to help open Cain's eyes and help him realize God knows everything—thoughts, words, attitudes, and actions.

God's questions sometimes shine a light on unbelief, too. In Genesis, God asked Sarah why she laughed when God said she would have a child even though she was an old woman. In Exodus, God asked questions of Moses when Moses was too frightened to believe God could speak through him to Pharaoh or use him to lead the Israelites. In Numbers, God questioned the Israelites about their unbelief despite His miraculous provisions for them as they left Egypt.

God, in the form of Jesus, asked His followers, "Who do you say I am?" (Matthew 16:15, NIV). Considering that question helped Jesus' disciples reevaluate their priorities. Answering it solidified their faith for a lifetime.

worth thinking about

▶ **God sometimes** uses questions like parents do, asking children the reason for their actions. In such instances, God usually vindicates Himself and His actions after a series of questions.

▶ **In the Book of Job,** God questioned Satan about his activity on earth and cautioned Job to brace himself because He was going to ask him some tough questions, too.

▶ **God uses questions** to help reveal His ways to His people. When God wanted to replace Saul as king of Israel, God questioned Samuel about his loyalties to God's ways.

There are times when God asks nothing of his children except silence, patience, and tears.
Charles Seymour Robinson

Readers who enjoyed this book will also enjoy

100 Answers to 100 Questions About God's Promises

100 Answers to 100 Questions About Loving Your Husband

100 Answers to 100 Questions About Loving Your Wife

100 Answers to 100 Questions About Prayer

100 Answers to 100 Questions to Ask Before You Say "I Do"